MY HAPPY PLACE

Art Therapy Coloring Book

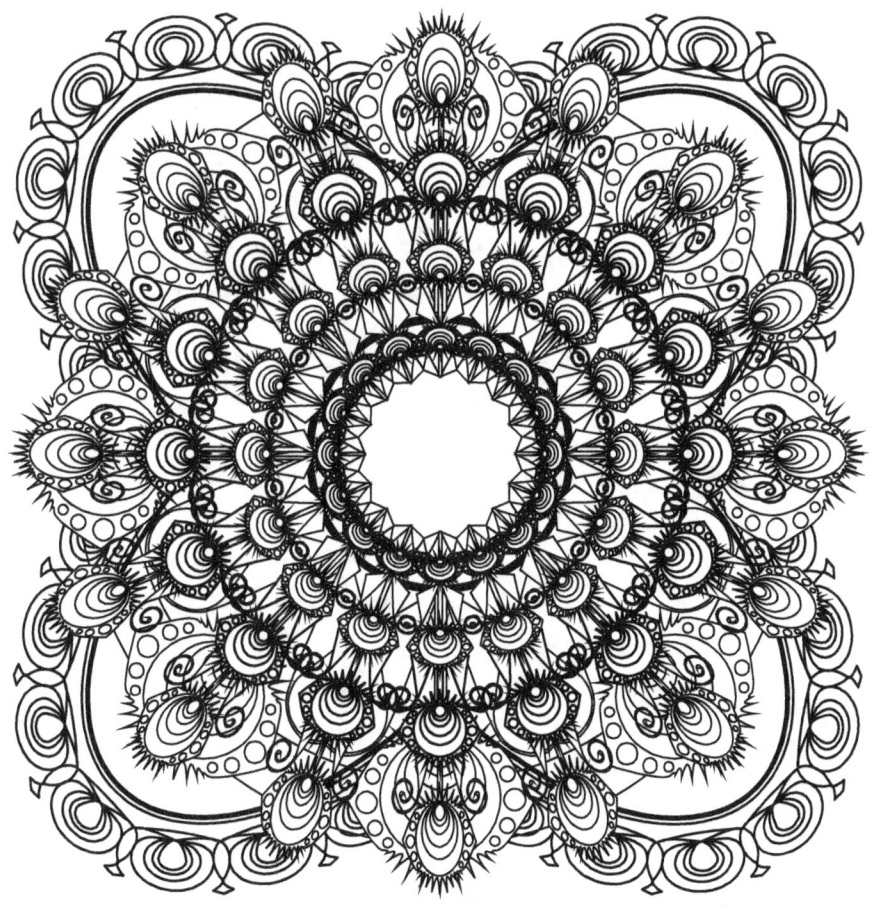

Tammy Groves Thornton

ISBN-13: 978-1523277155

ISBN-10: 1523277157

Welcome to the wonderful world of coloring!

Coloring is not just fun...it is calming, therapeutic and the perfect antidote to life's everyday stresses.

Using your imagination, my drawings, and whatever medium you want - crayons, markers, color pencils, pens, etc. - you can create a beautiful and unique new world of stillness and peace.

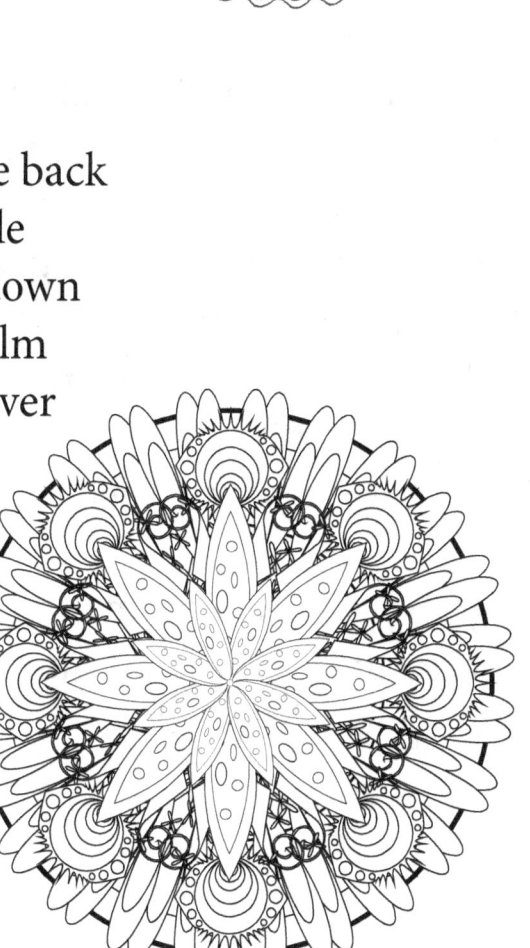

My Happy Place contains more than 50 mandalas and intricate patterns just waiting to be filled with vibrant colors. It is designed to unlock your imagination and help you relax and express yourself.

Don't miss the words of inspiration on the back of each illustration, sure to make you smile and feel grateful. I encourage you to jot down things that you are grateful for. With a calm mind and grateful heart, I hope you discover your Happy Place too!

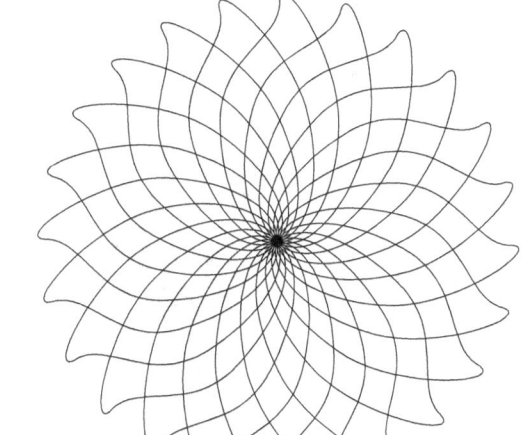

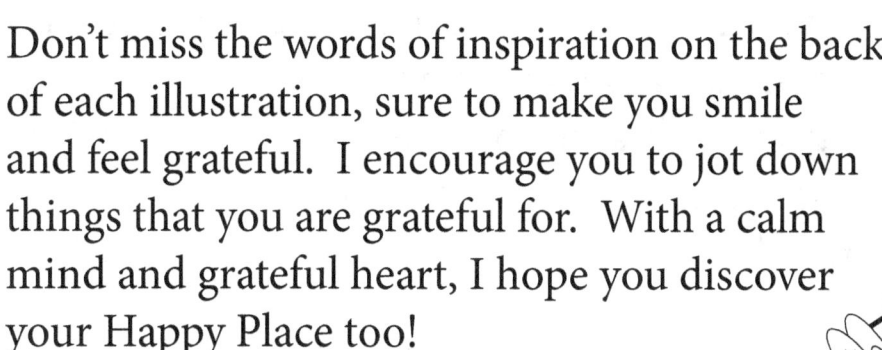

The word Mandala means "circle". A Mandala represents wholeness, the search for completeness, and self-unity. The mandala appears to us in all aspects of life, such as the Earth, the Sun, the Moon and more obviously the circles of life encompassing friends, family and communities. Mandalas are circular designs symbolizing the notion that life is never ending. Mandalas are used for meditation purposes allowing the individual meditating to become one with the universe.

When coloring your mandala, I encourage you to choose colors that appeal to you, colors that relax you, colors that calm you, or colors that make you happy. And if you can't decide, here are some suggestions to get you started:

RED for strength, high energy and passion
PINK for love, intuition and the feminine
ORANGE for creativity, transformation, self-awareness, and intuition
YELLOW for learning, wisdom, laughter, and happiness
GREEN for physical healing, love of nature, and caring
BLUE for emotional healing, inner peace, and meditation
PURPLE for all things spiritual
WHITE for spiritual focus
BLACK for mystery, deep thinking and individuality

So grab your crayons, markers, color
pencils, and pens, find a quiet spot,
and happy coloring!!!

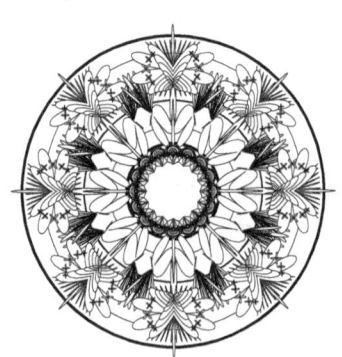

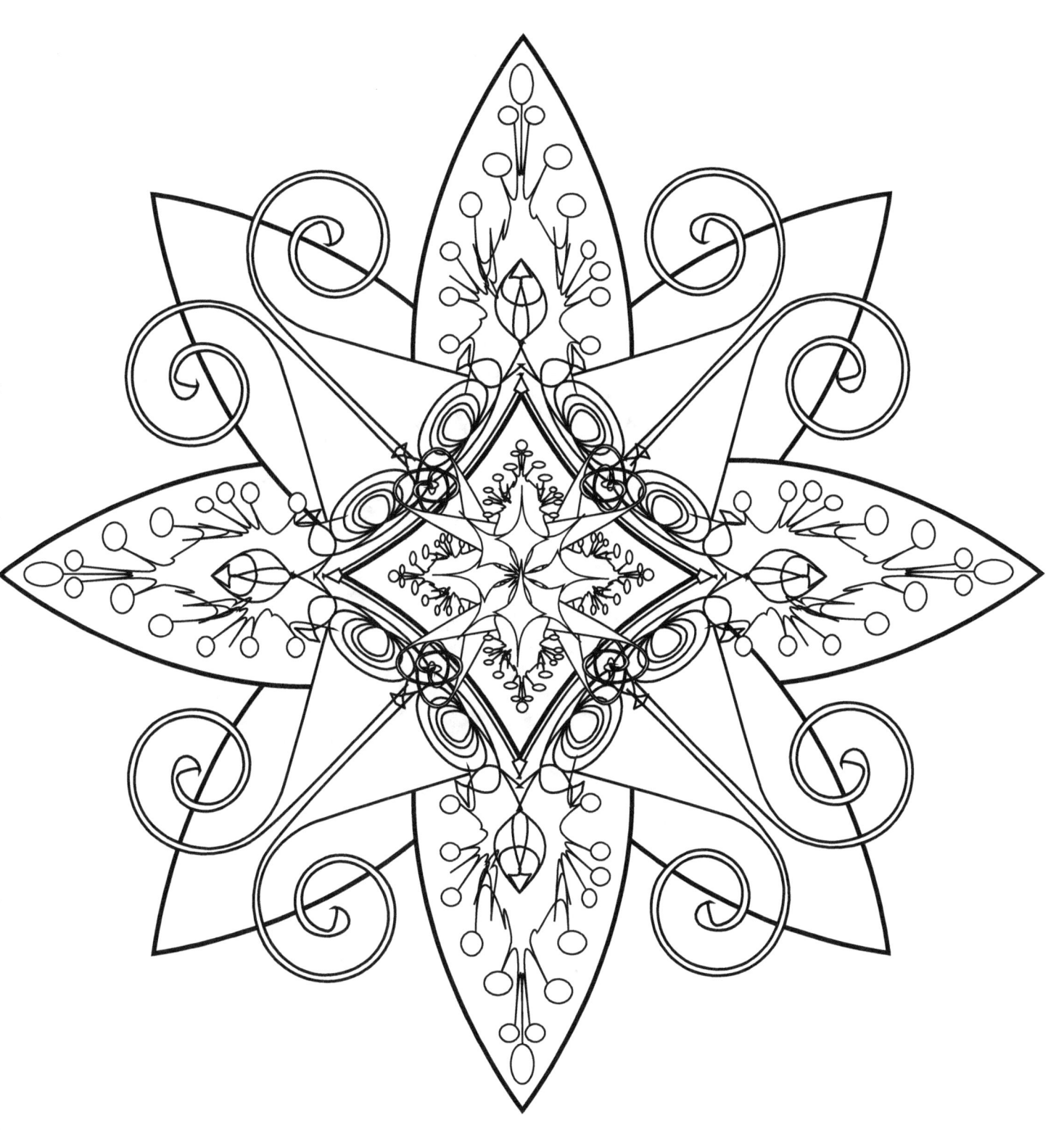

Dream Big Dream Big Dream Big Dream Big Dream Big Dream Big Dream Big Dream Big Dream Big Dream Big

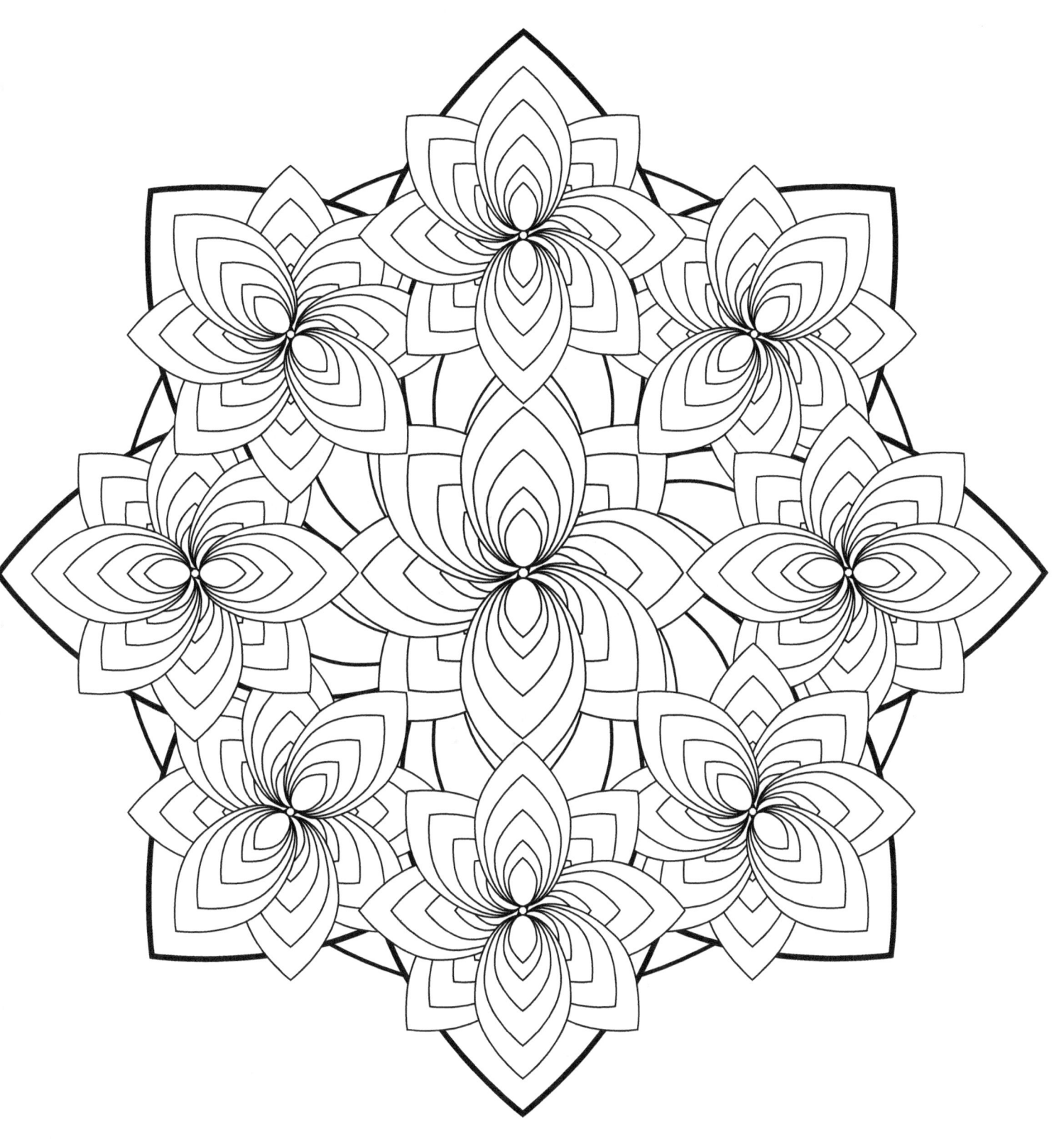

Be Brave Be Brave Be Brave Be Brave Be Brave Be Brave

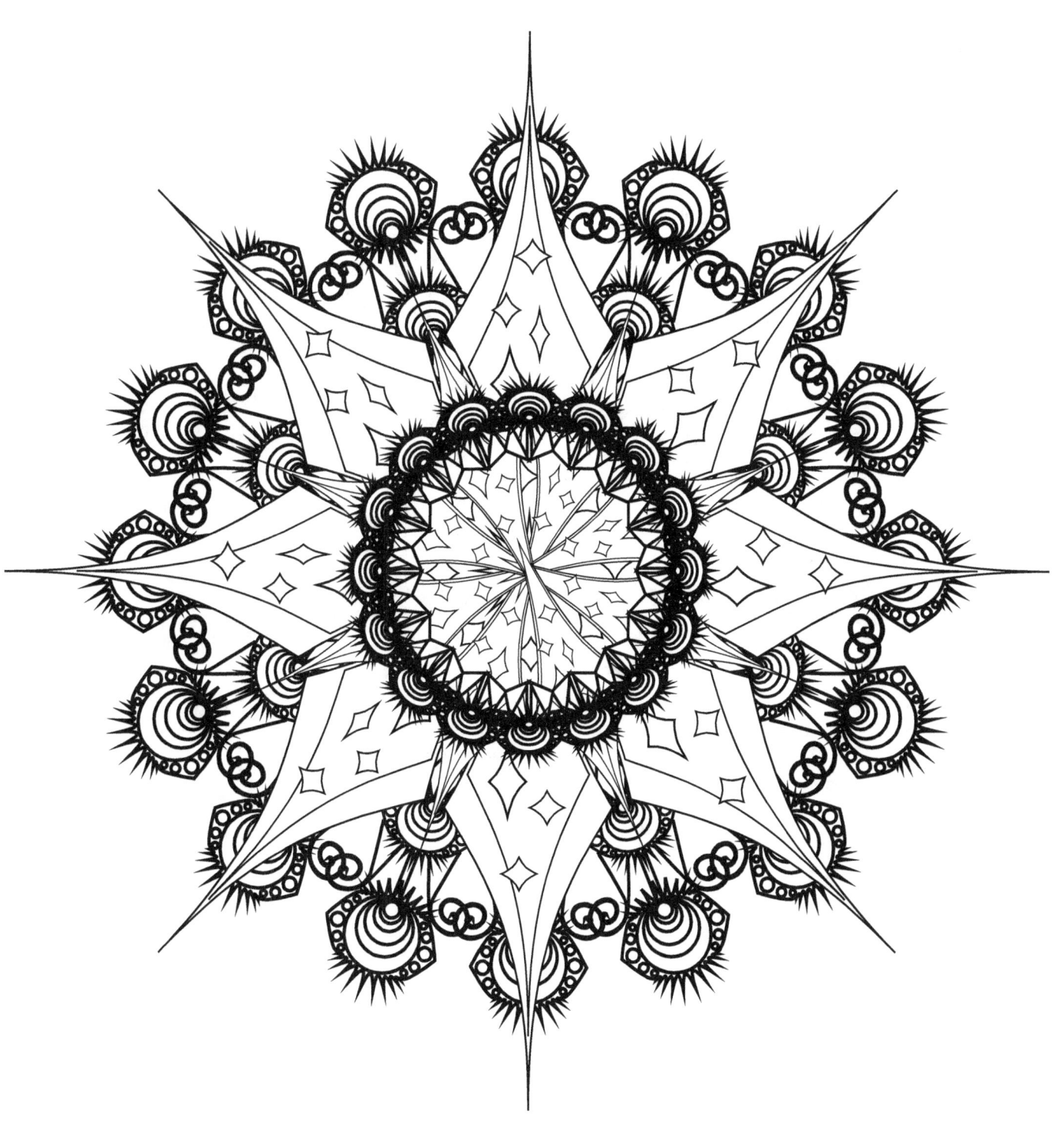

Be-YOU-TiFUL Be-YOU-TiFUL Be-YOU-TiFUL Be-YOU-TiFUL Be-YOU-TiFUL

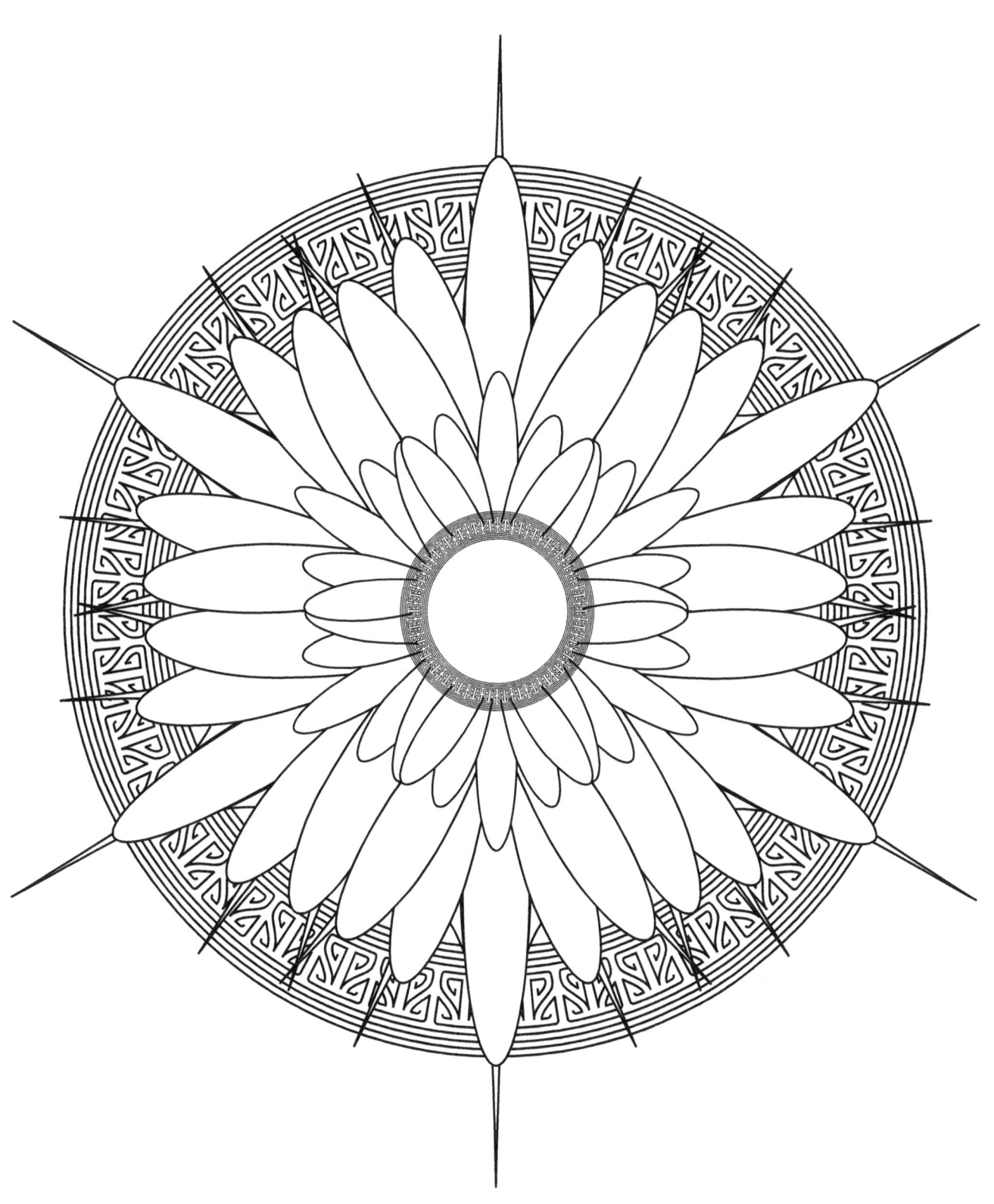

Be Courageous Be Courageous Be Courageous Be Courageous Be Courageous

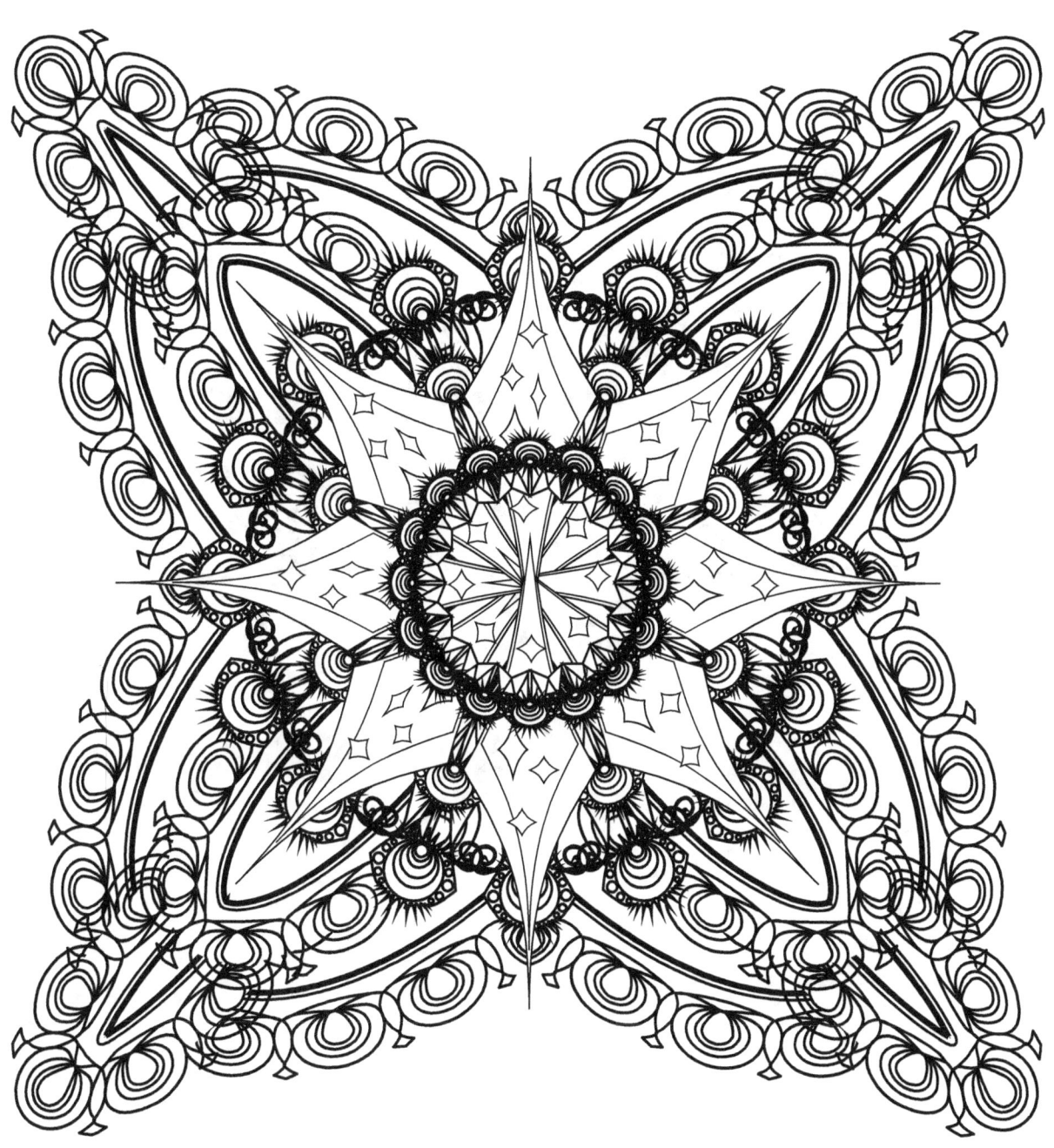

Follow your Heart Follow your Heart Follow your Heart Follow your Heart Follow your Heart

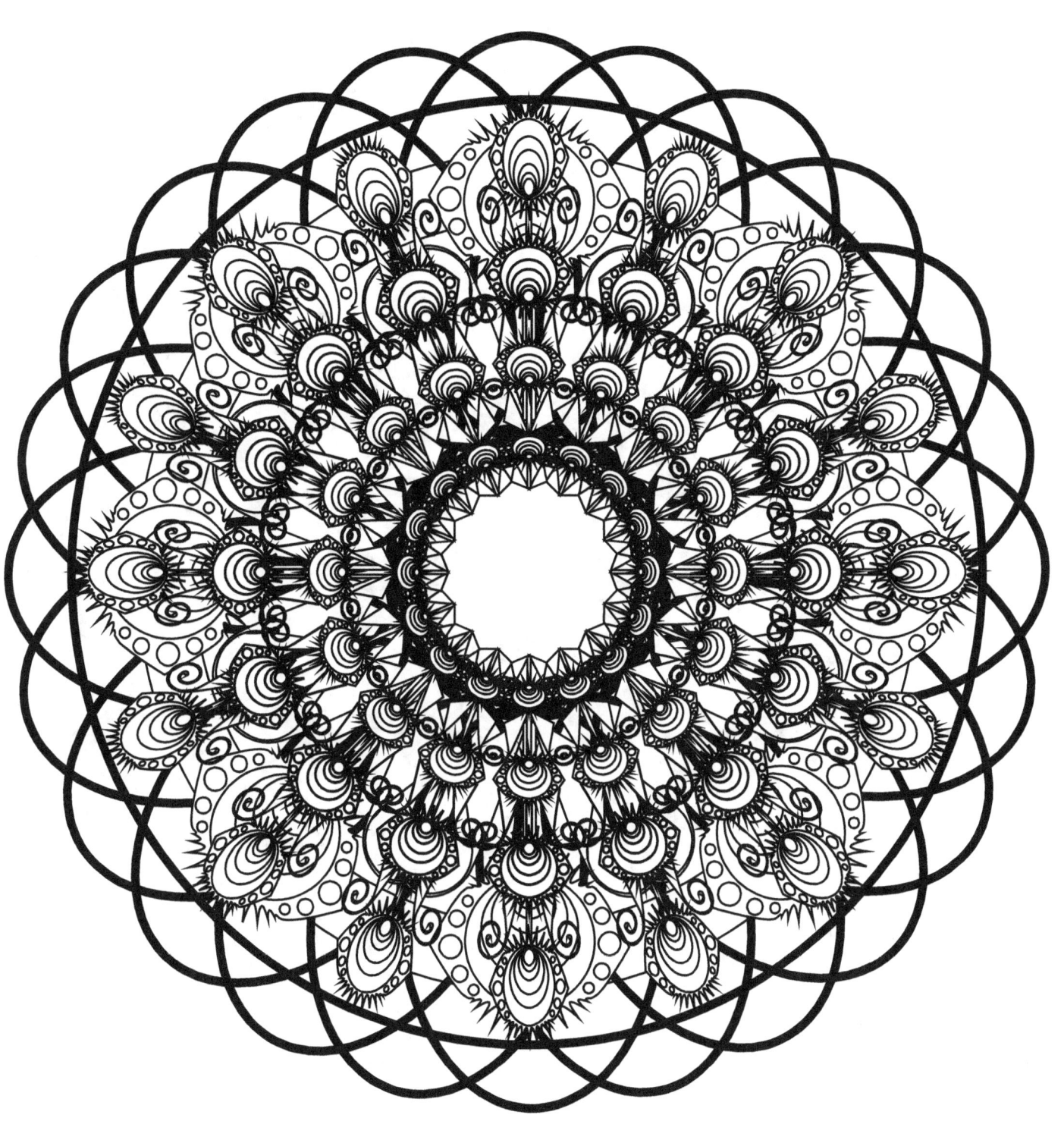

INSPIRE INSPIRE INSPIRE INSPIRE INSPIRE INSPIRE INSPIRE INSPIRE

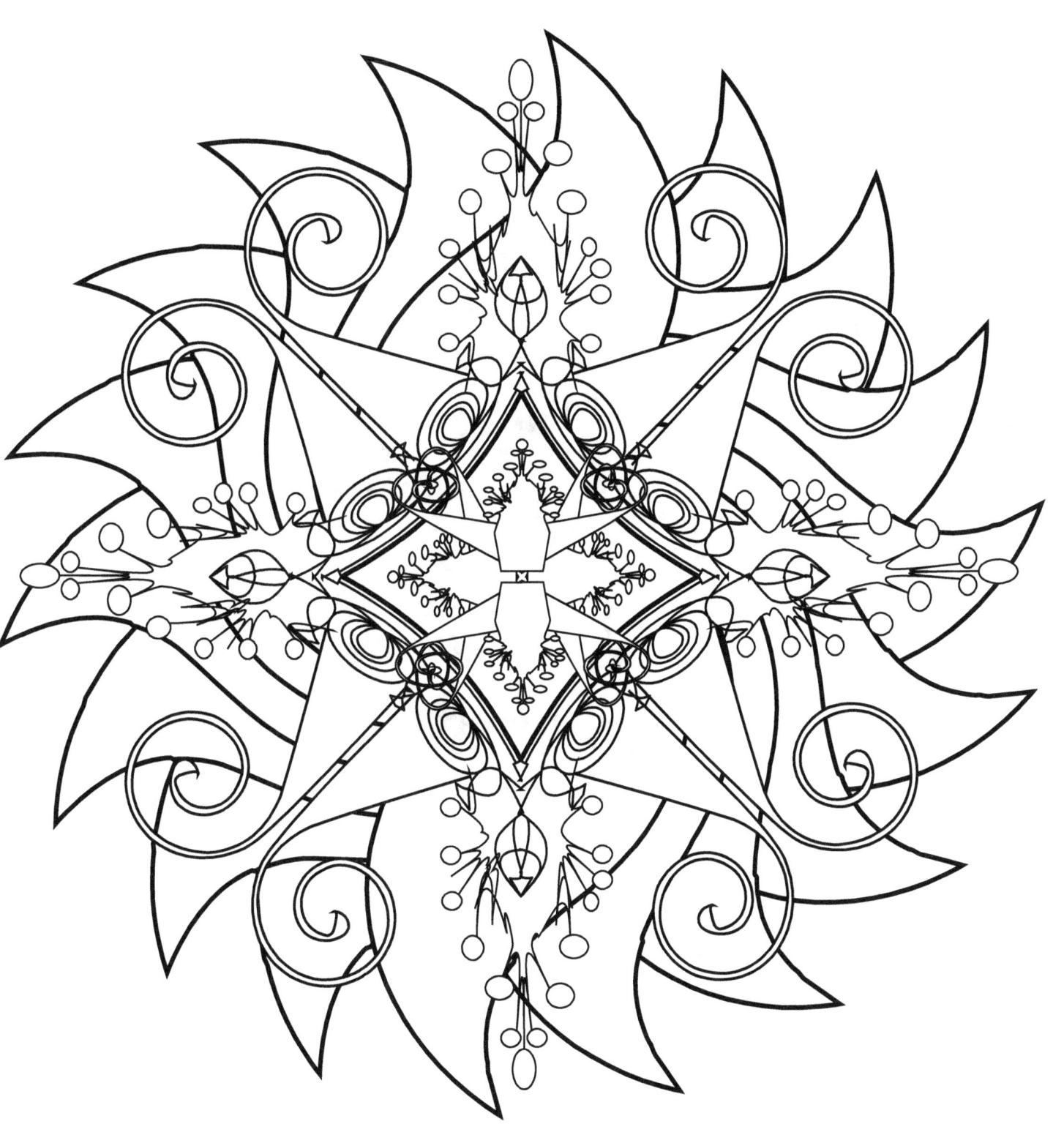

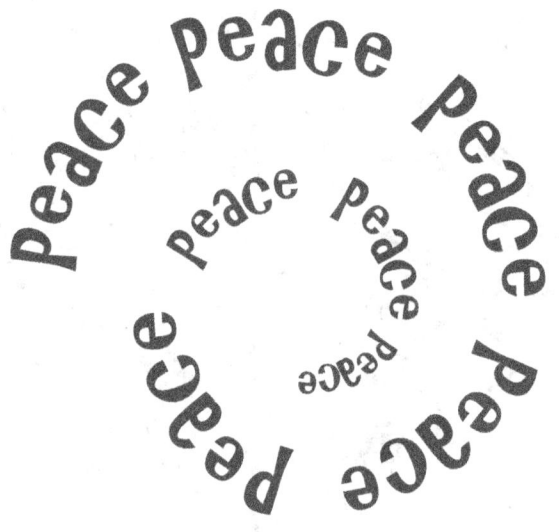

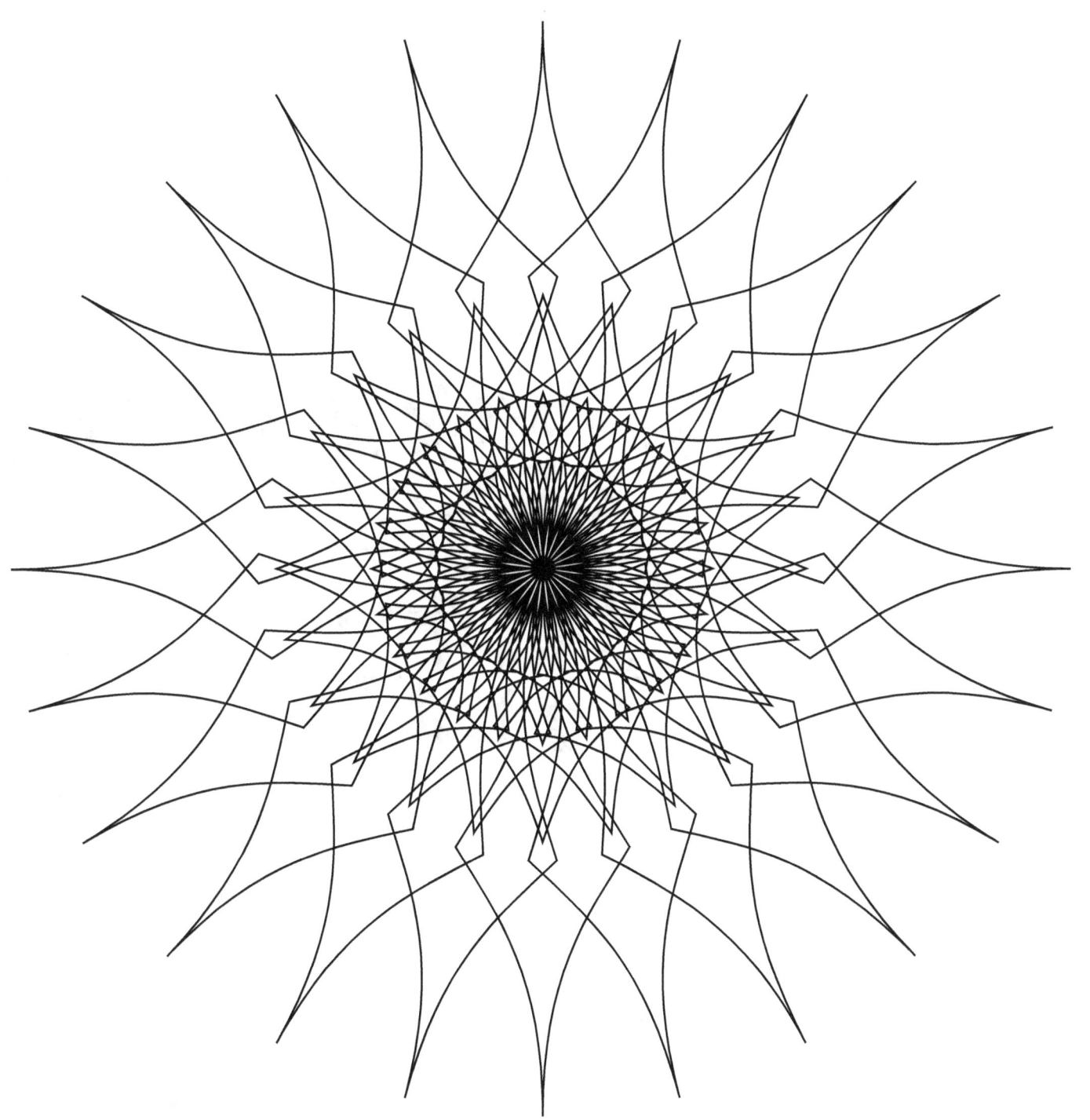

LOVE LOVE LOVE LOVE LOVE LOVE LOVE LOVE LOVE LOVE

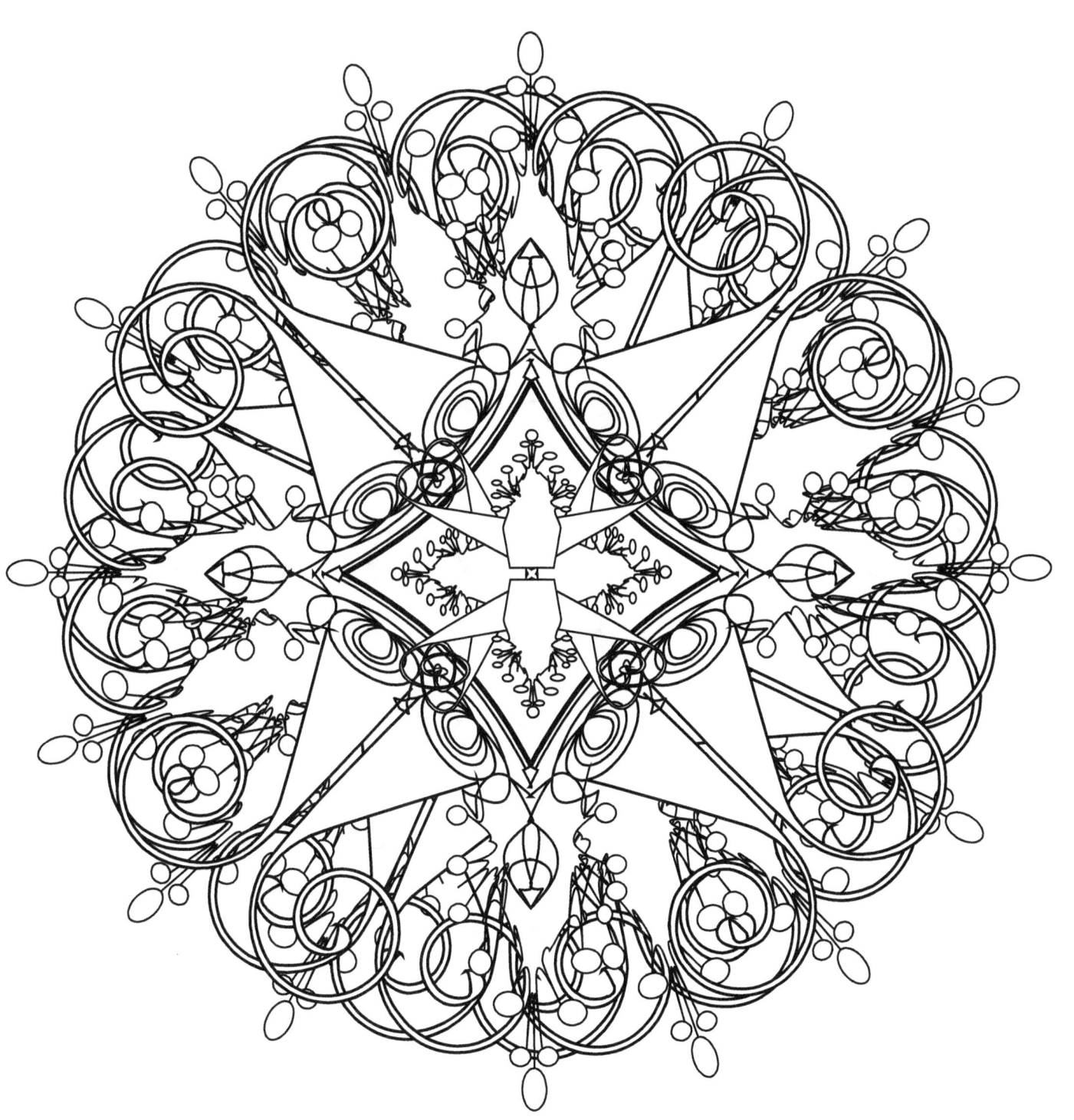

Love Never Fails Love Never Fails Love Never Fails Love Never Fails Love Never Fails

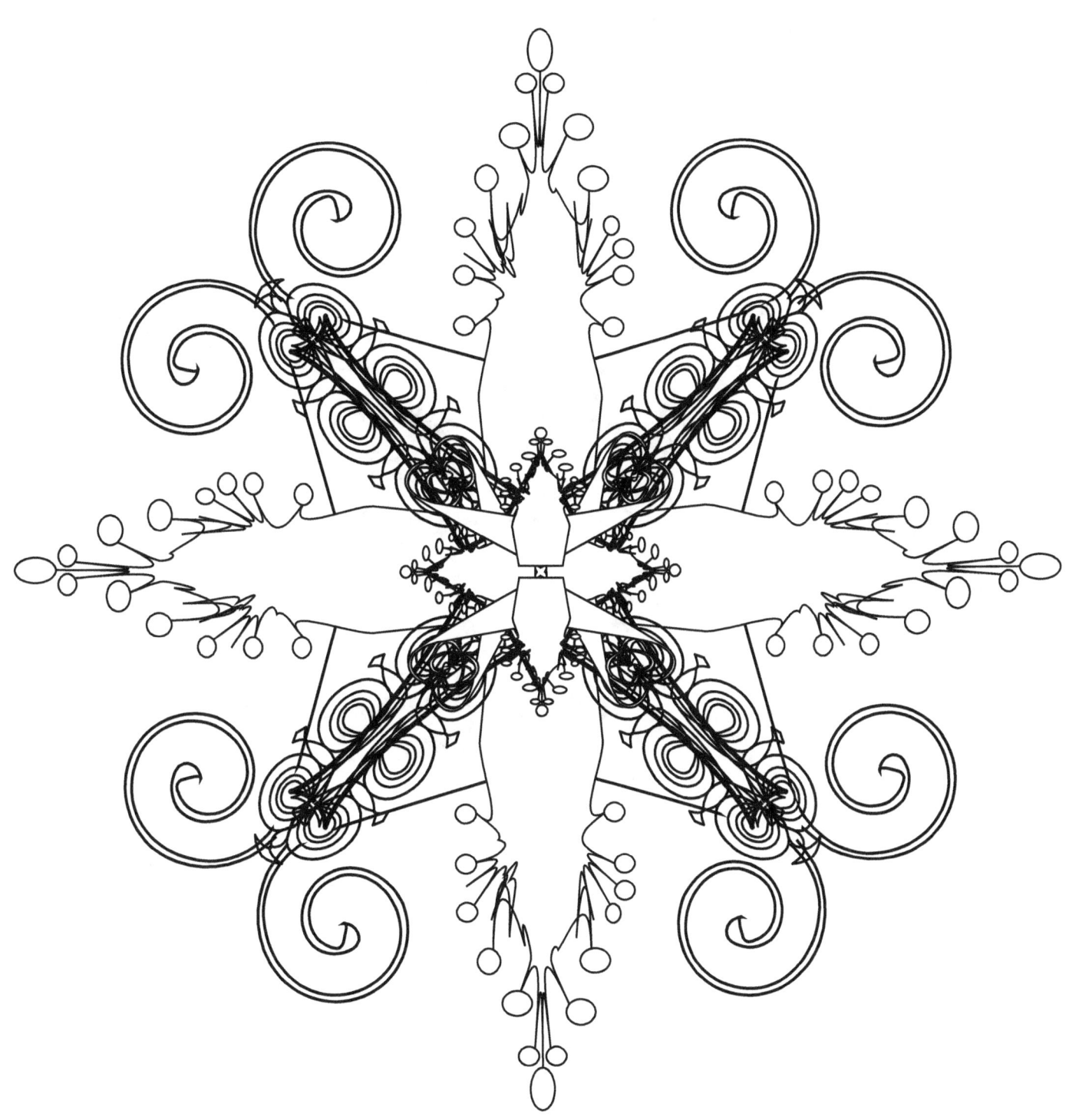

ALL GiRLS RoCK ALL GiRLS RoCK ALL GiRLS RoCK ALL GiRLS RoCK ALL GiRLS RoCK

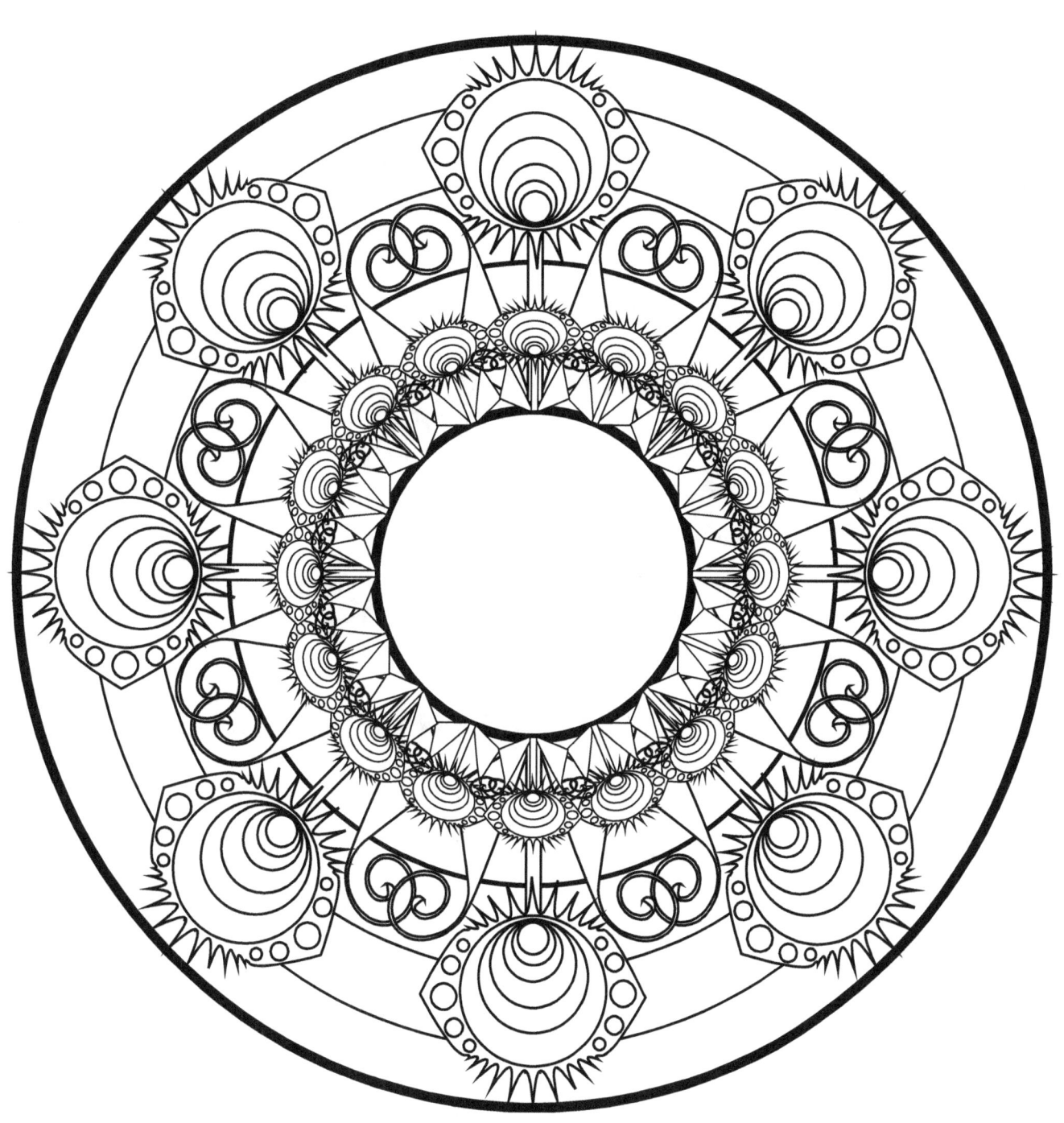

Amazing Grace Amazing Amazing Grace Amazing Grace Amazing Grace

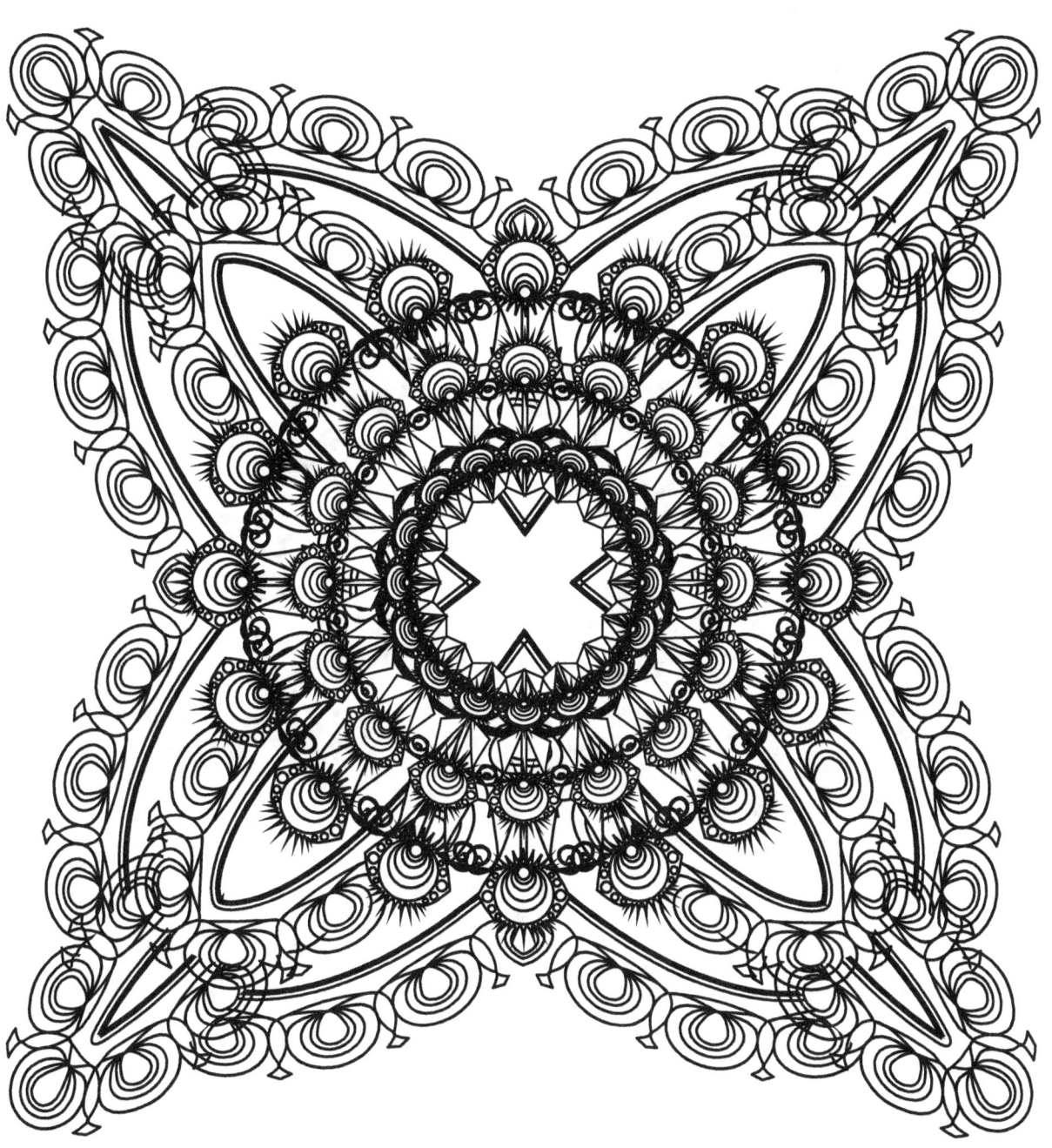

Celebrate everyday Beauty

Celebrate everyday Beauty

Celebrate everyday Beauty

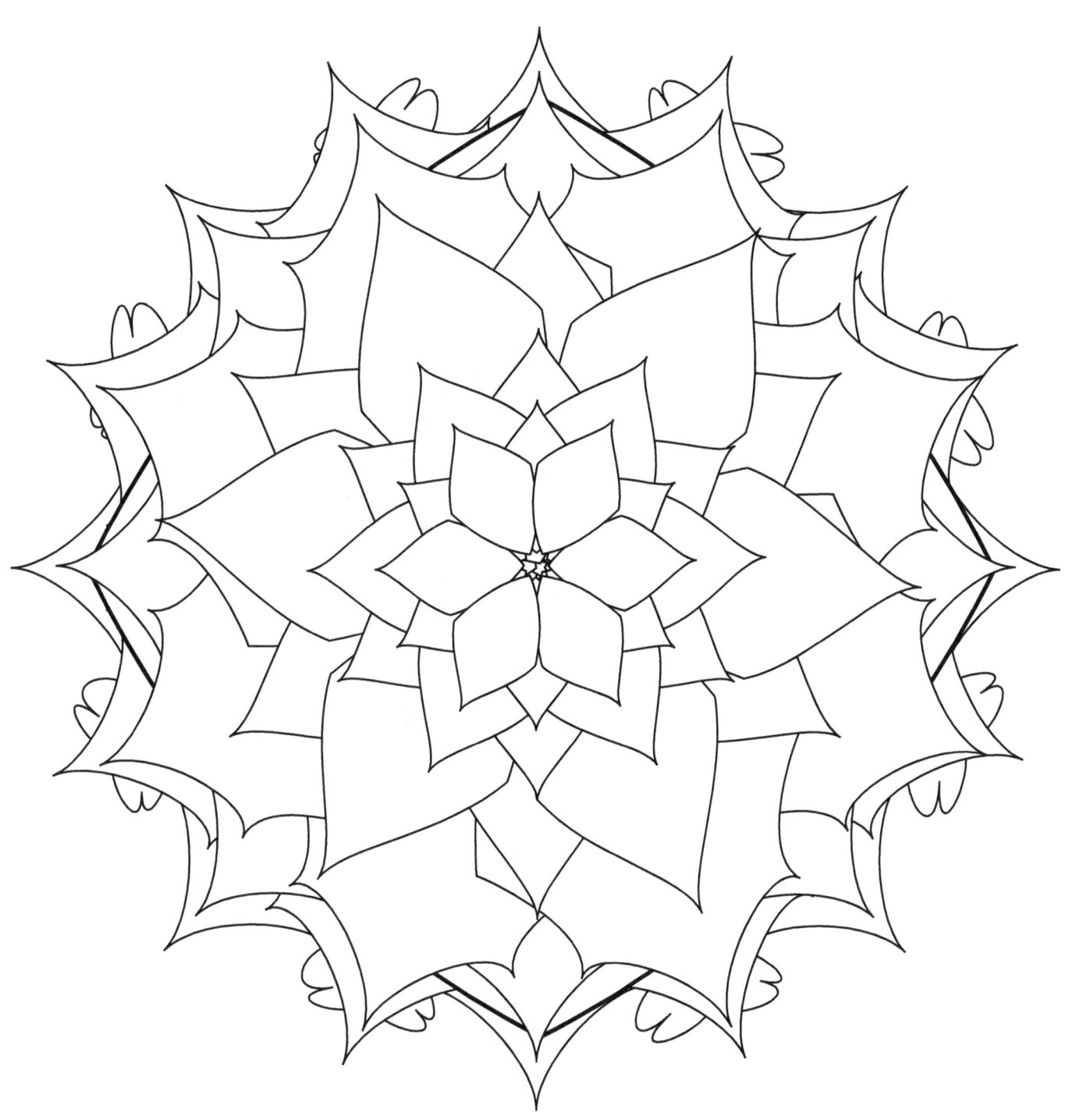

BeLieVe iN YourSeLF BeLieVe iN YourSeLF BeLieVe iN YourSeLF BeLieVe iN YourSeLF

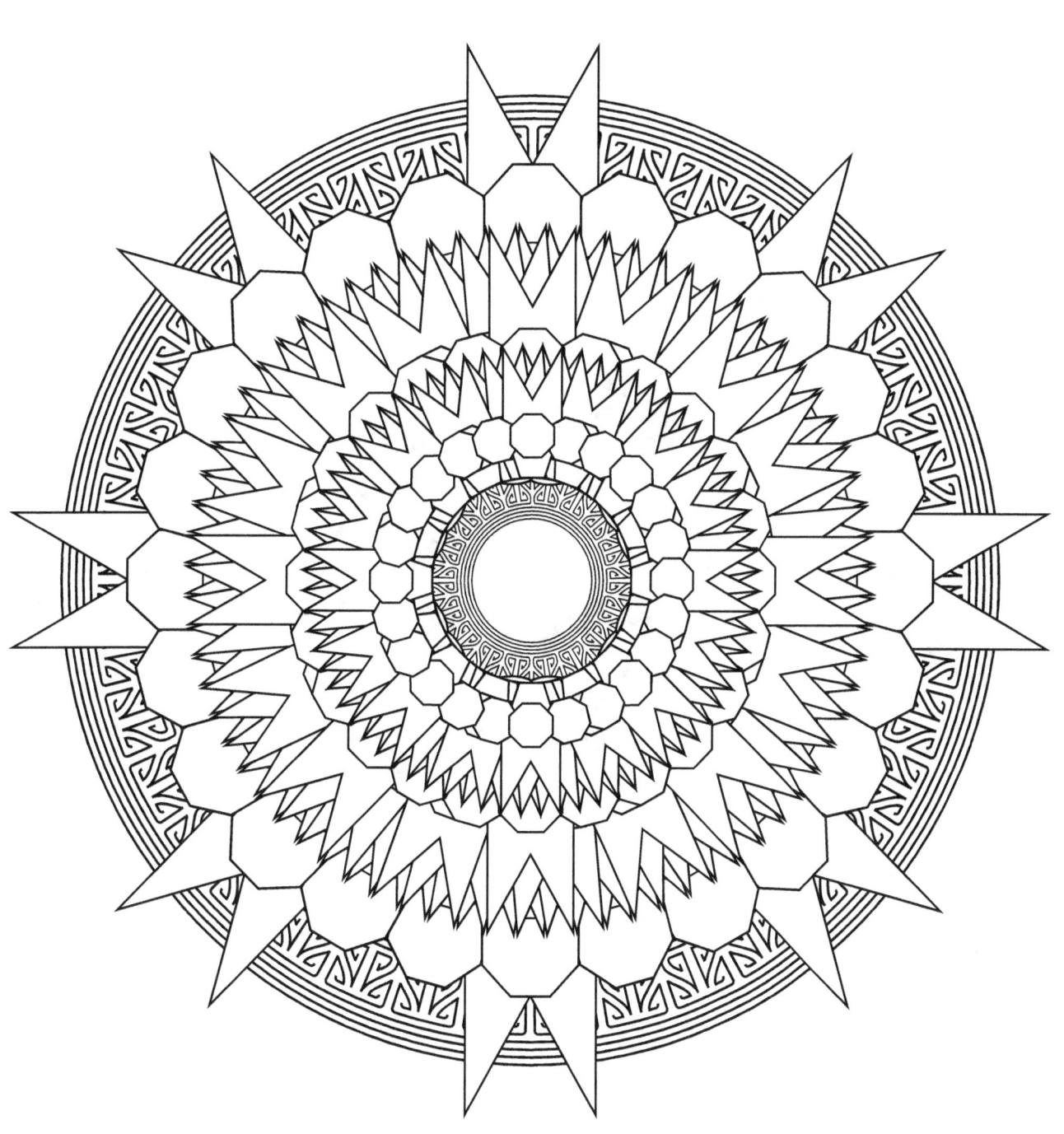

Dreams Do Come True Dreams Do Come True Dreams Do Come True Dreams

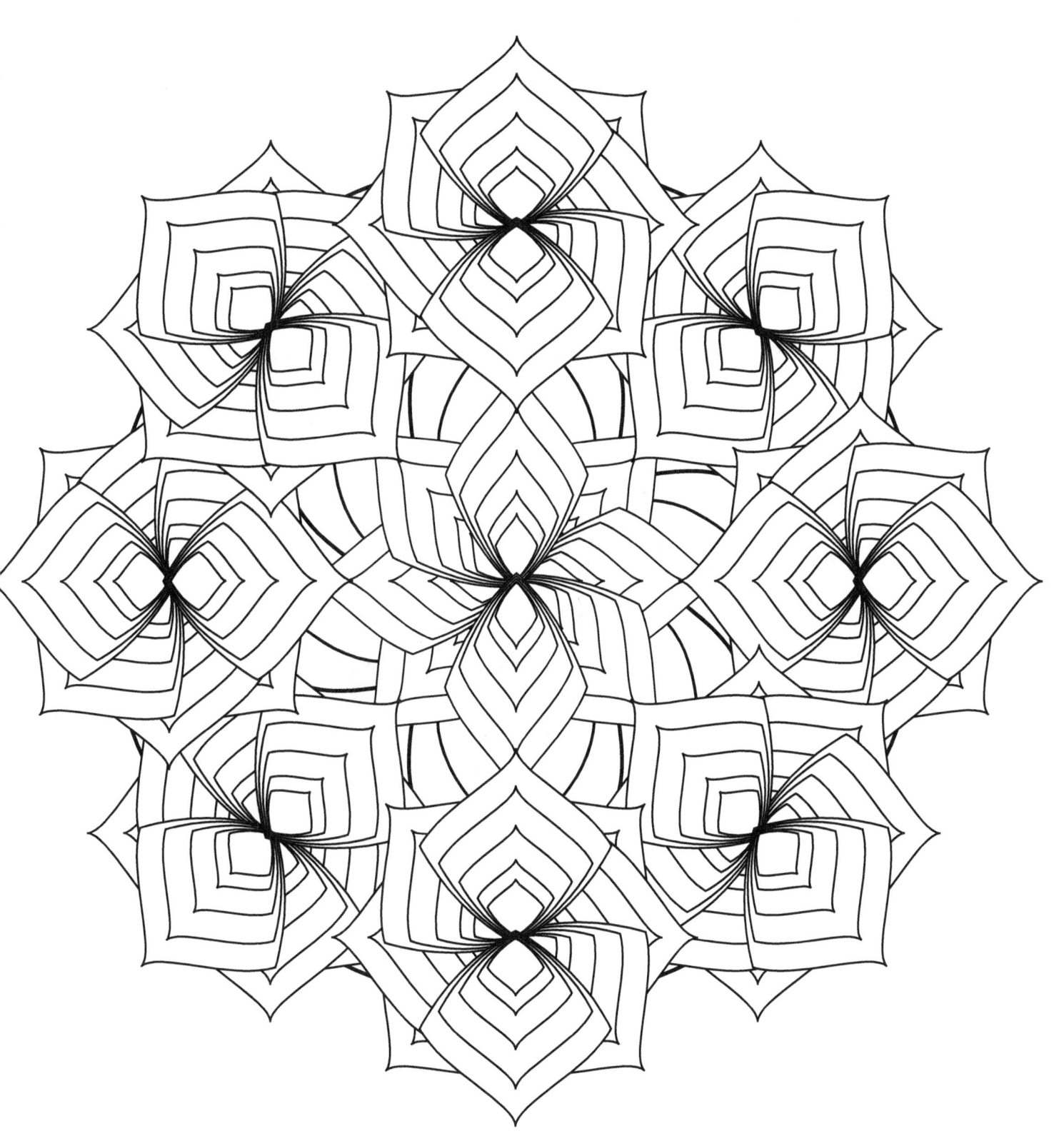

Encourage Encourage Encourage Encourage Encourage Encourage Encourage Encourage

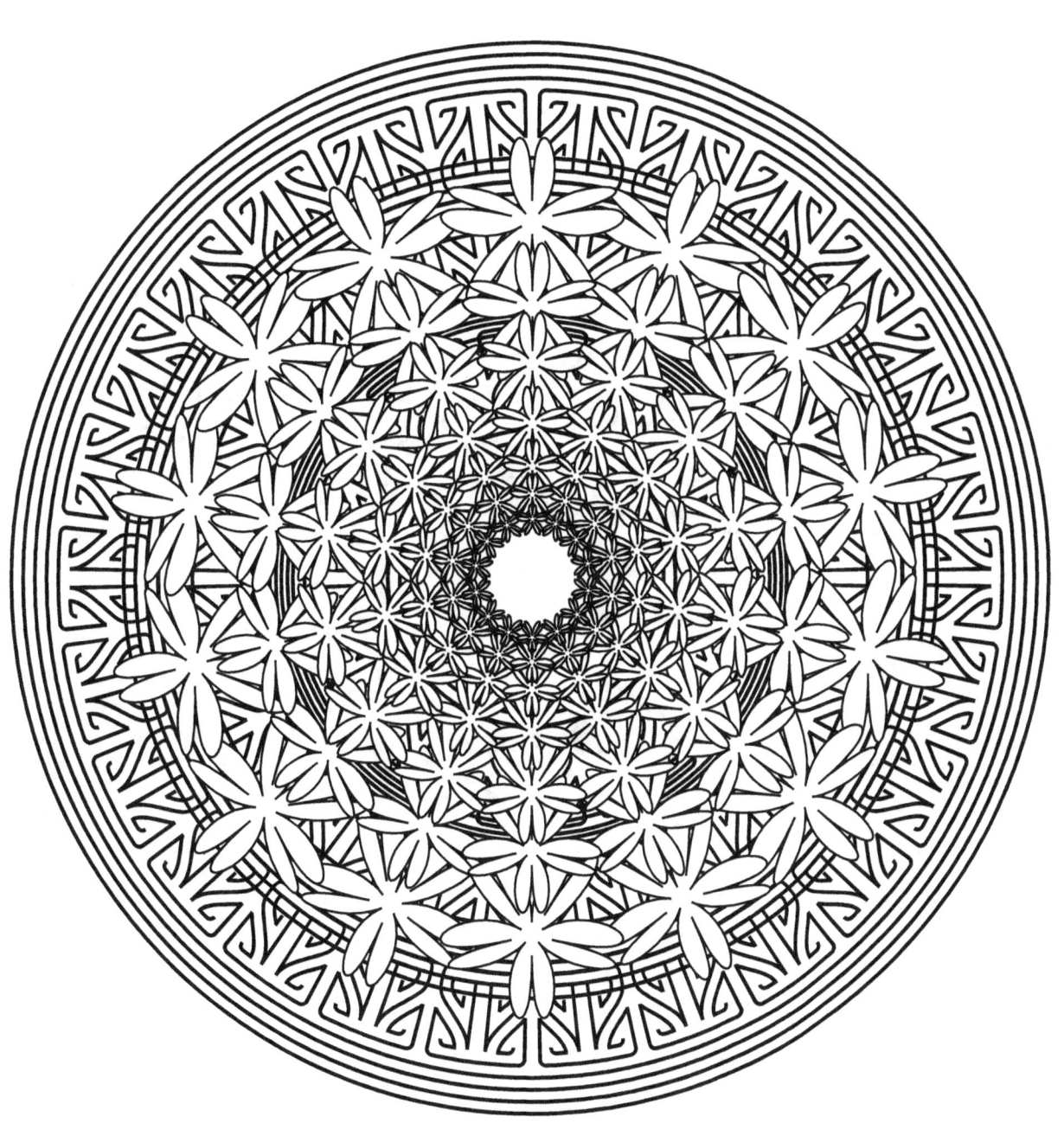

Be BoLd! Be BoLd! Be
BoLd! Be BoLd! Be BoLd! Be
BoLd! Be BoLd! Be BoLd!

_____

_____

_____

_____

_____

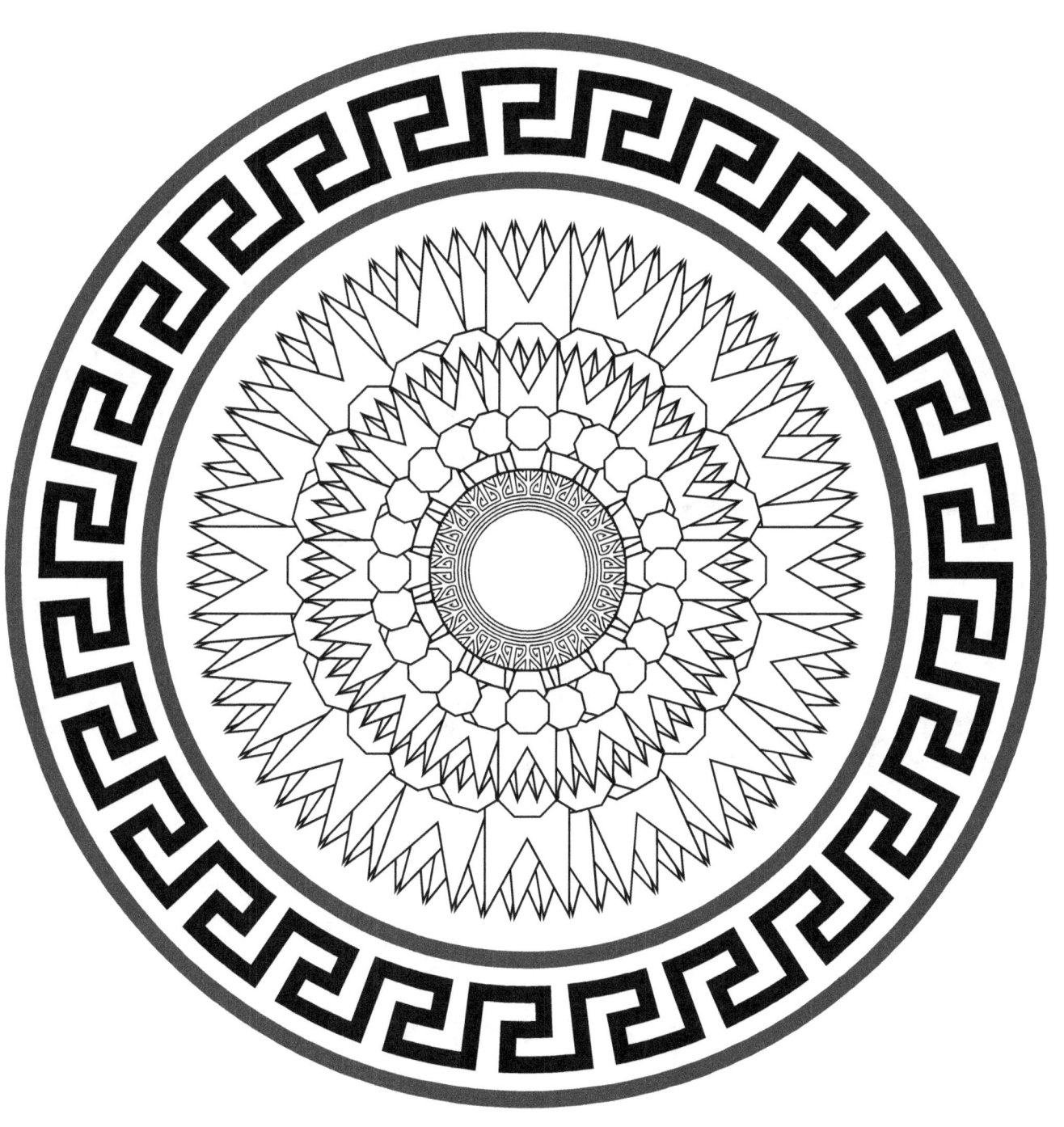

Live your passion Live your passion Live your passion Live your passion Live your passion

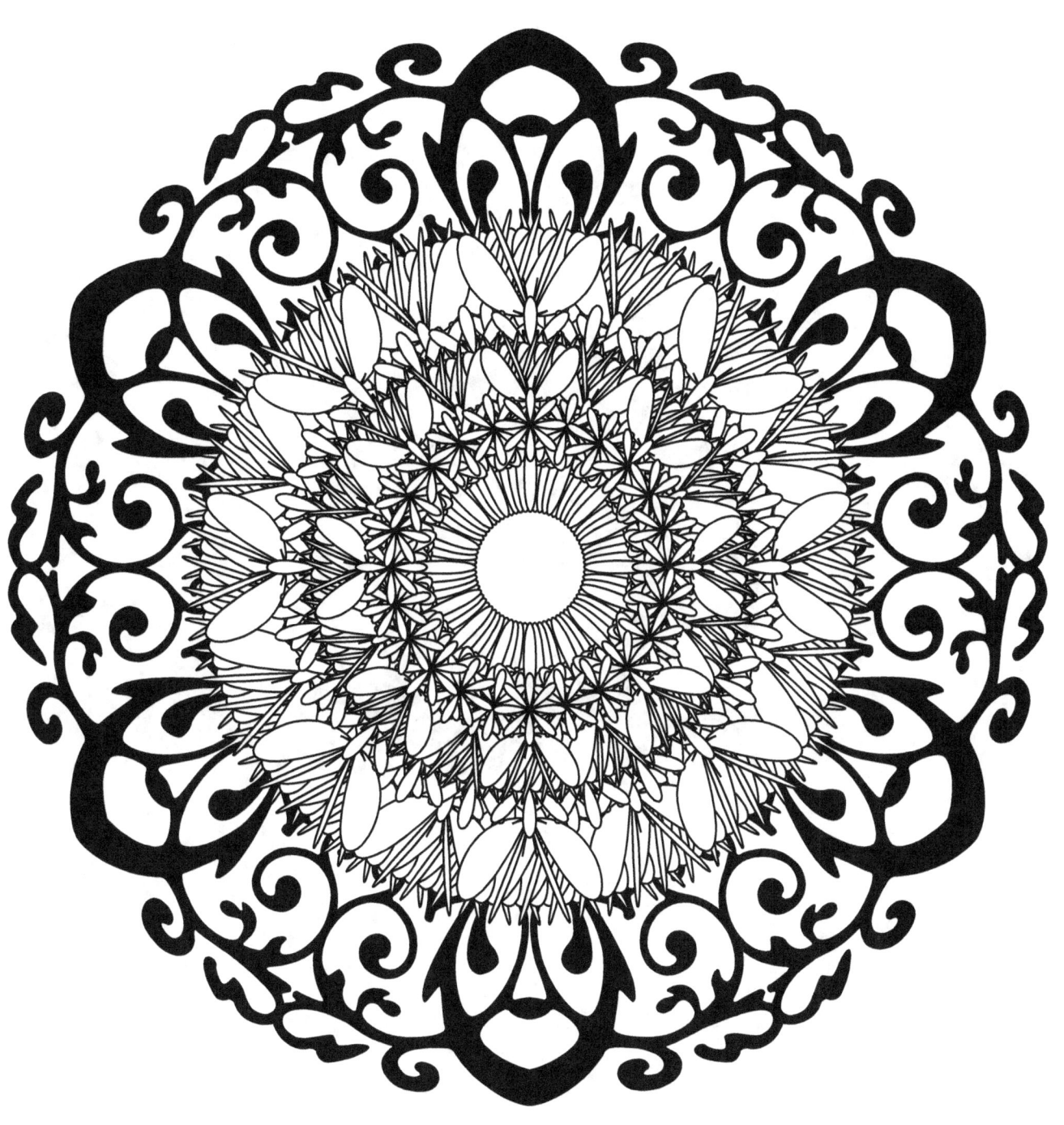

Never Stop Learning Learning Never Stop Never Stop Learning Never Stop

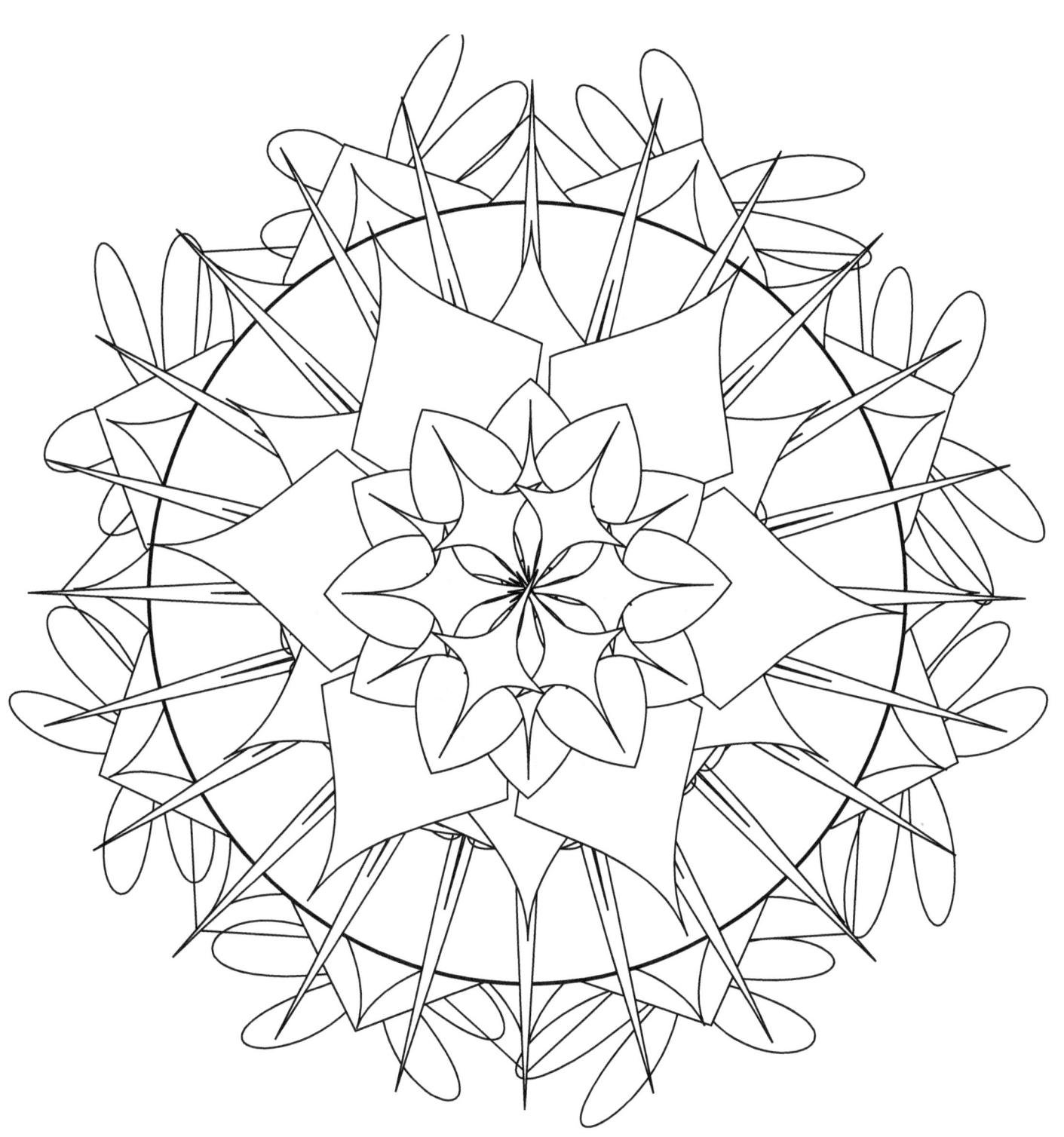

Teach Others Teach Others Teach Others Teach Others

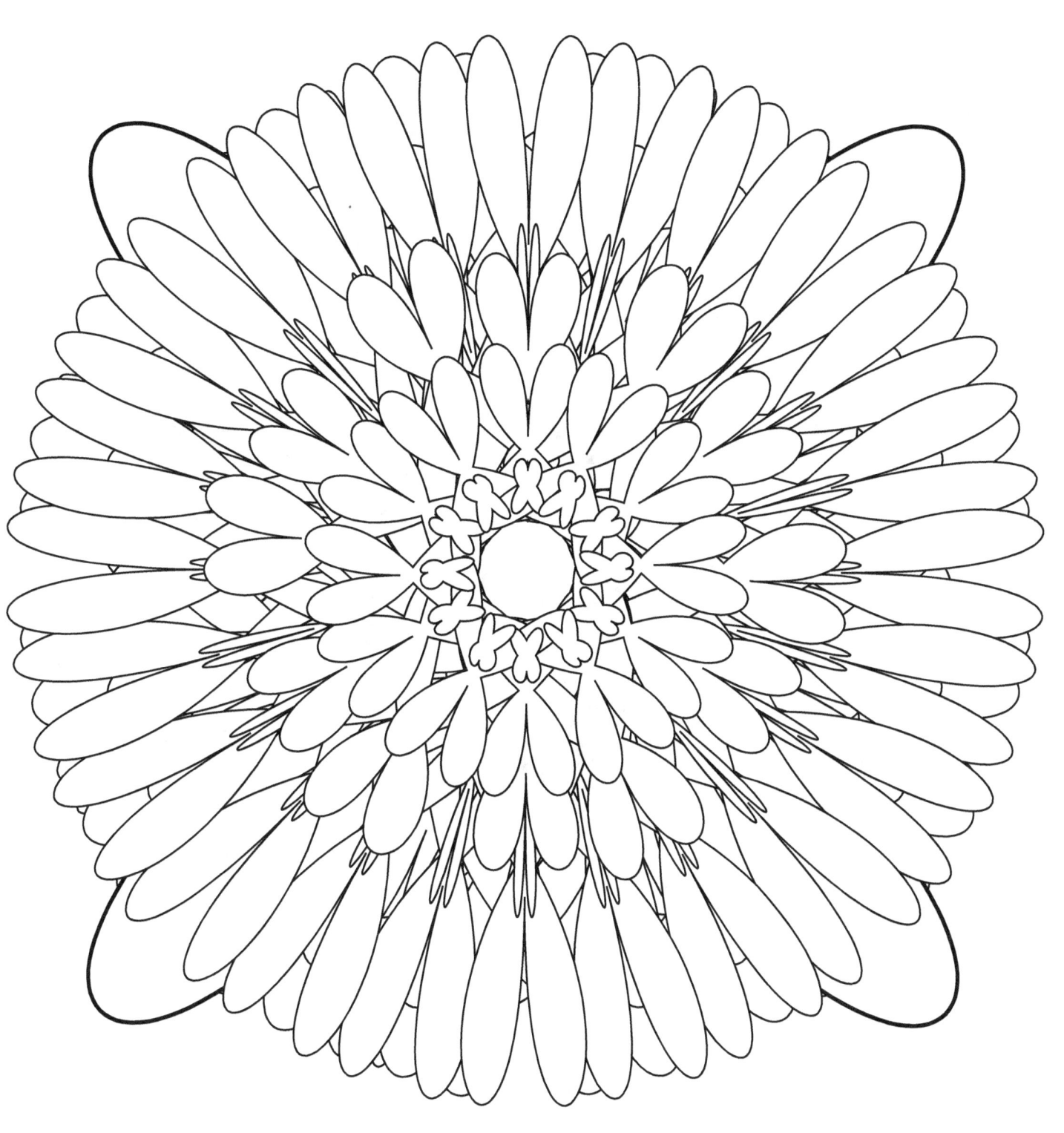

Stand Strong Stand Strong Stand Strong Stand Strong Stand Strong

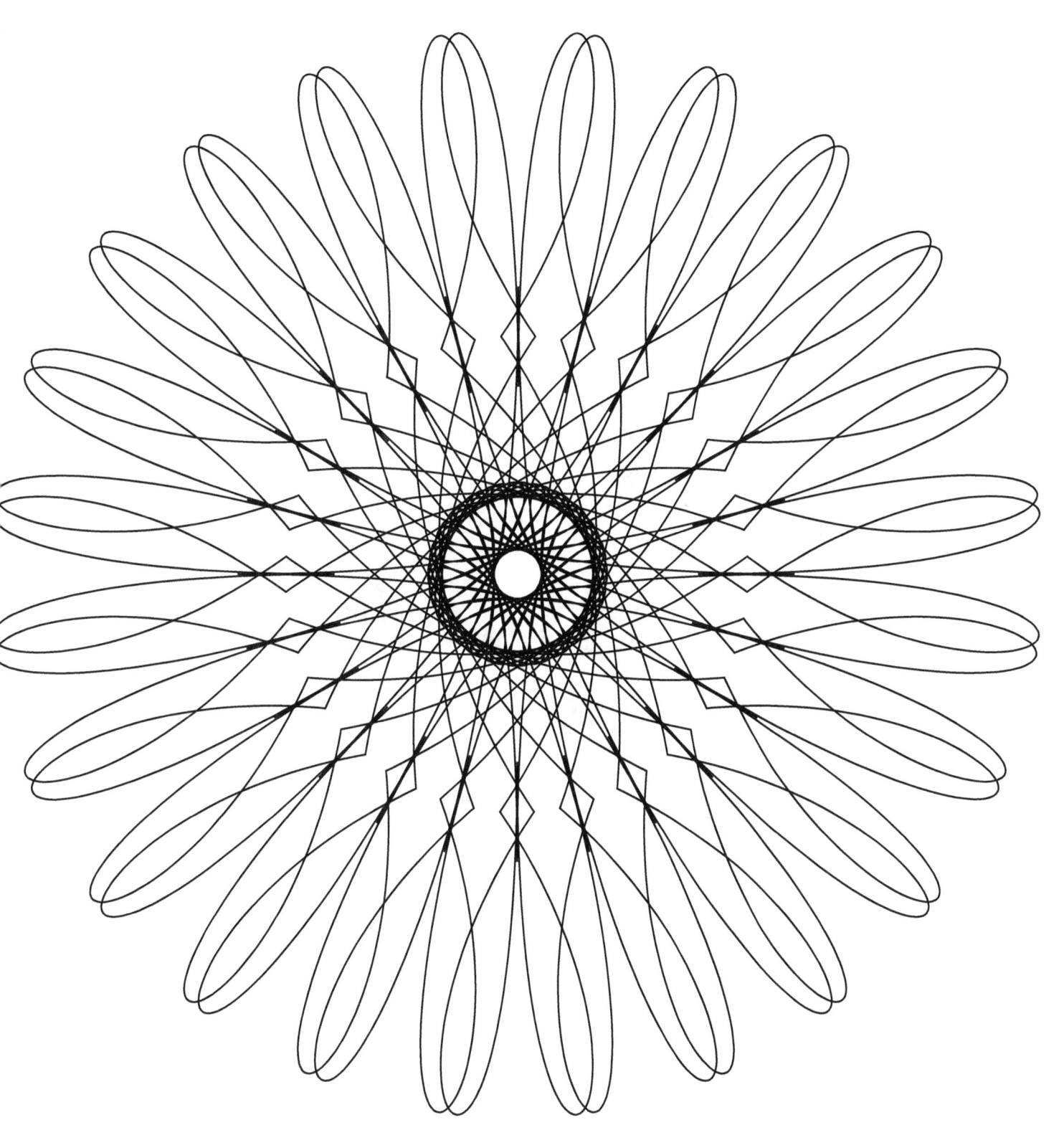

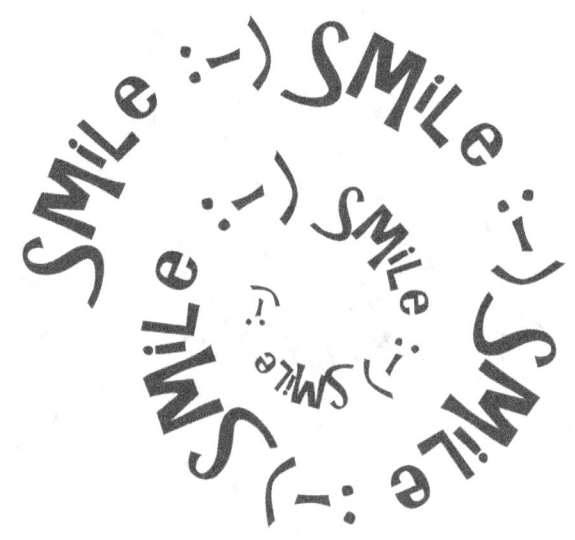

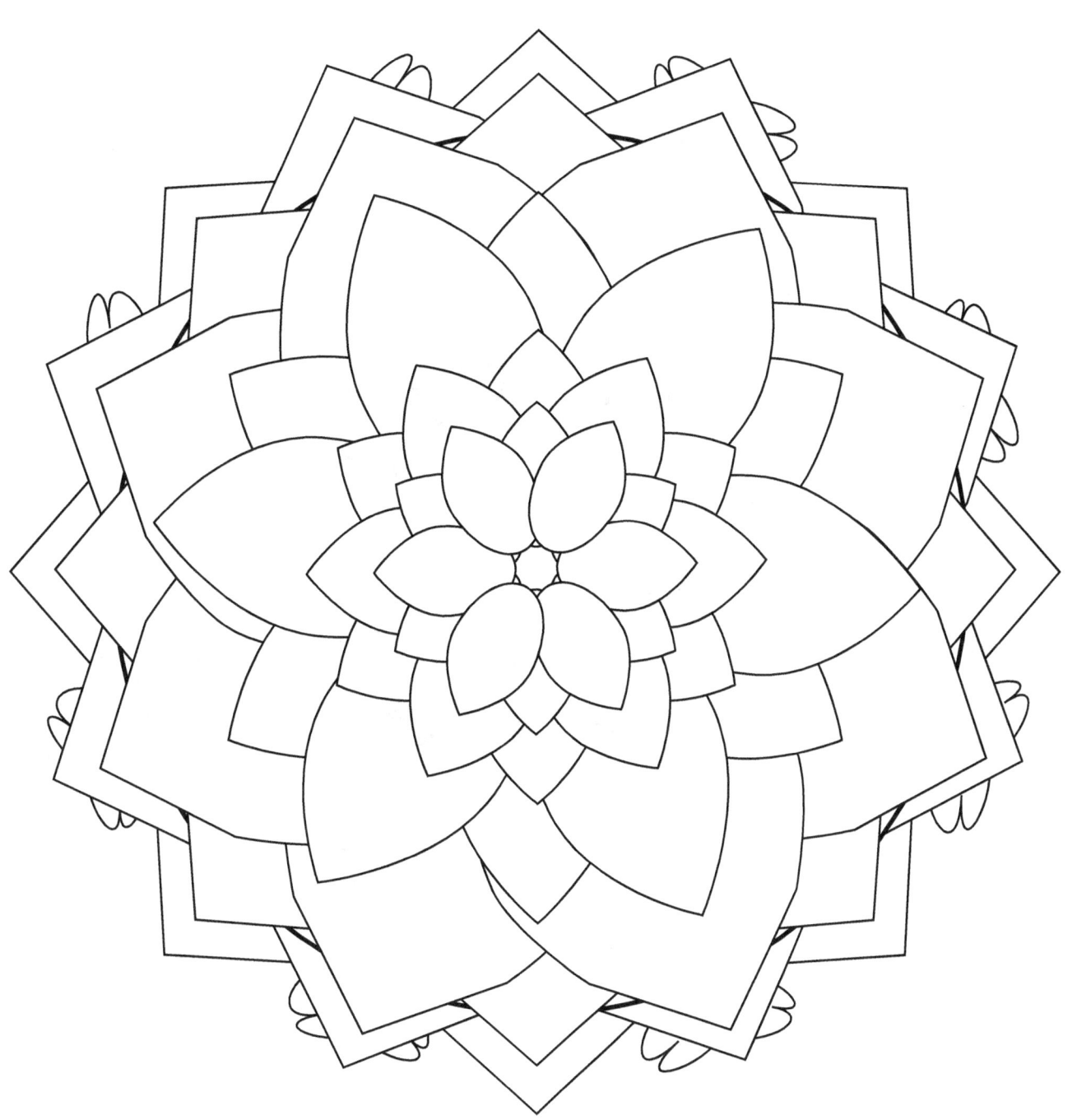

DeStiNY DeStiNy DeStiNy
DeStiNy
DeStiNy
DeStiNy
DeStiNy
DeStiNy
DeStiNy
DeStiNy

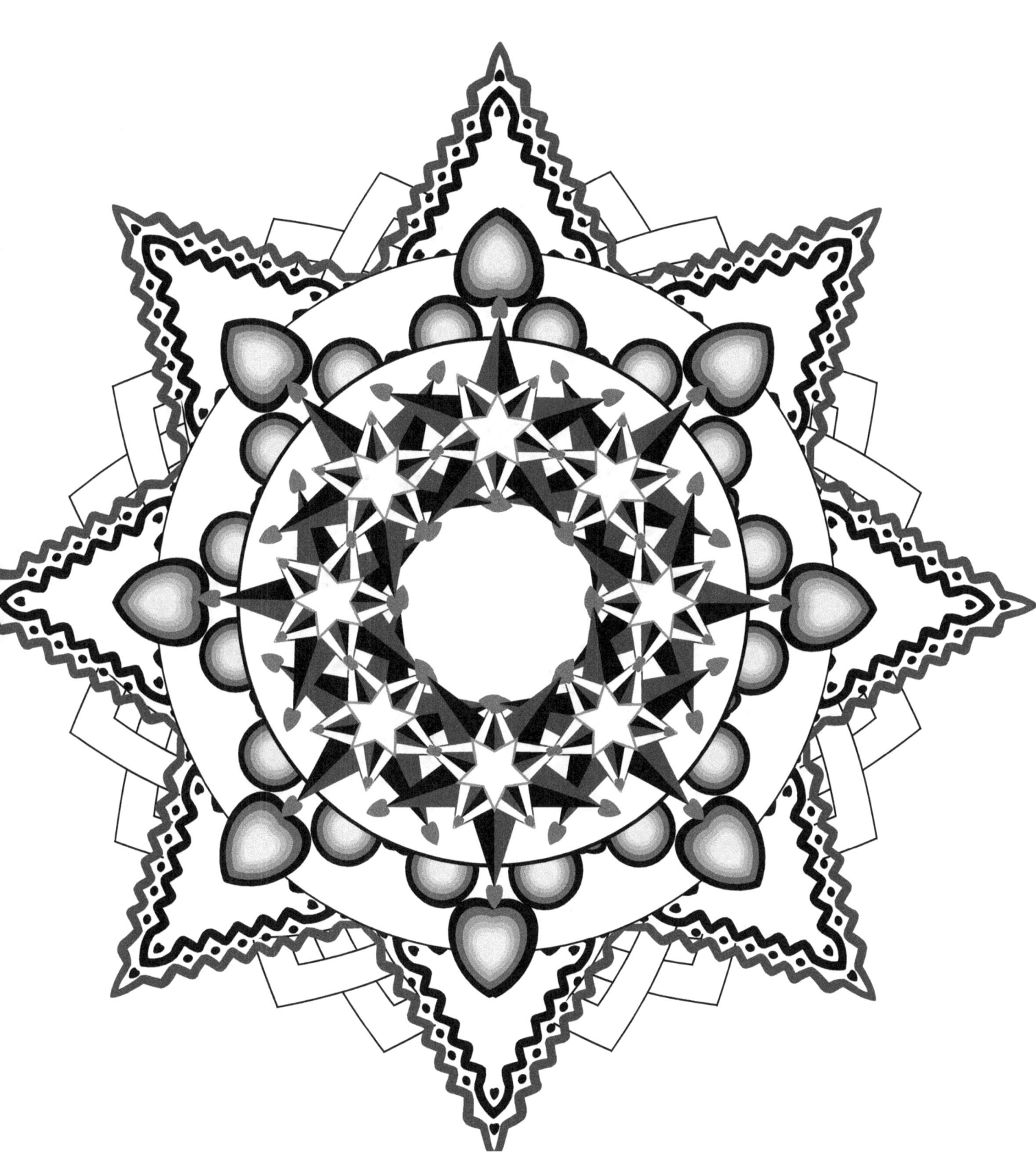

Dream your Dream your Dream your Dream your Dream your Dream your Dream your Dream

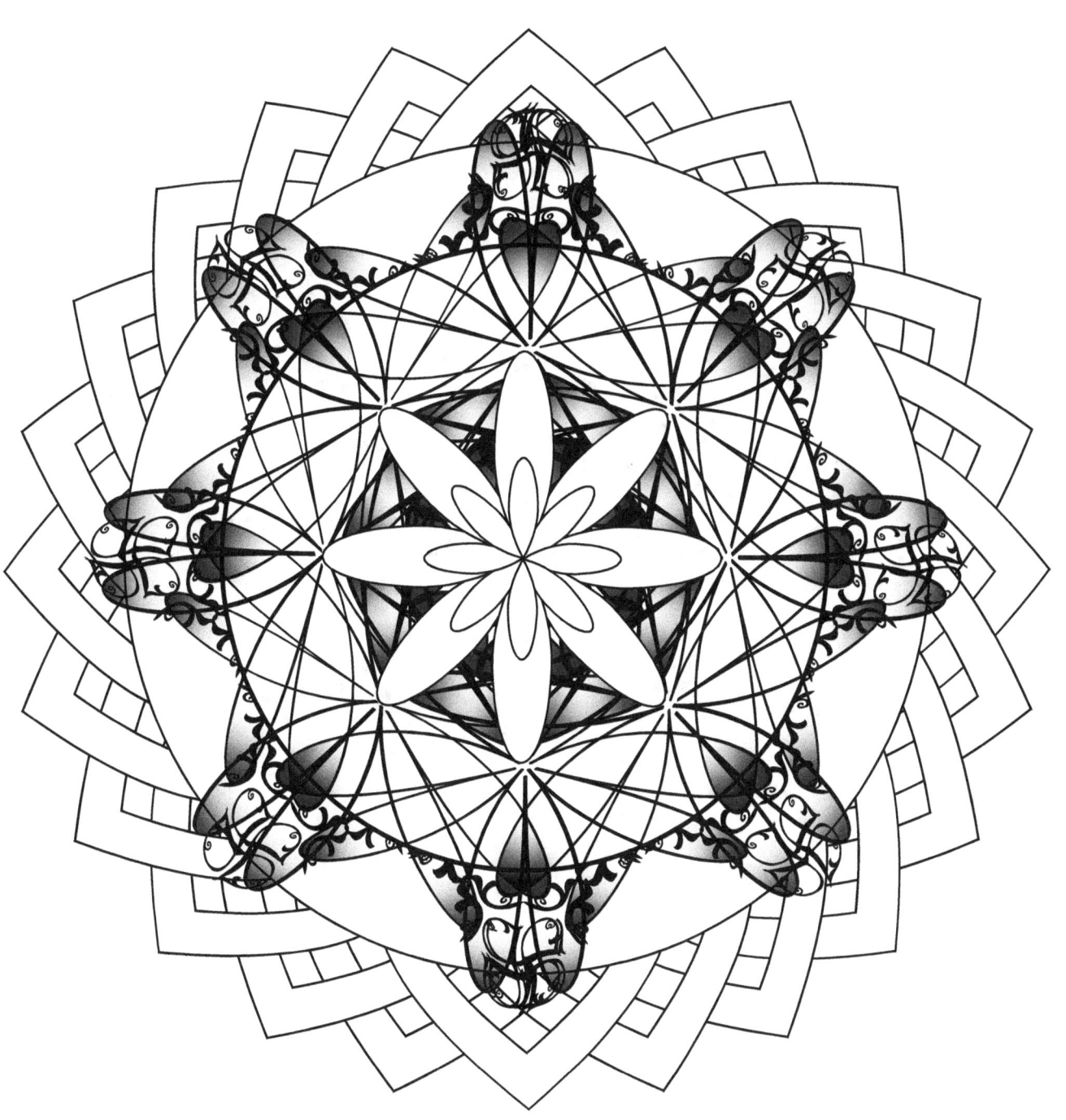

BeLieVe iN YourSeLF BeLieVe iN YourSeLF BeLieVe iN YourSeLF BeLieVe iN YourSeLF

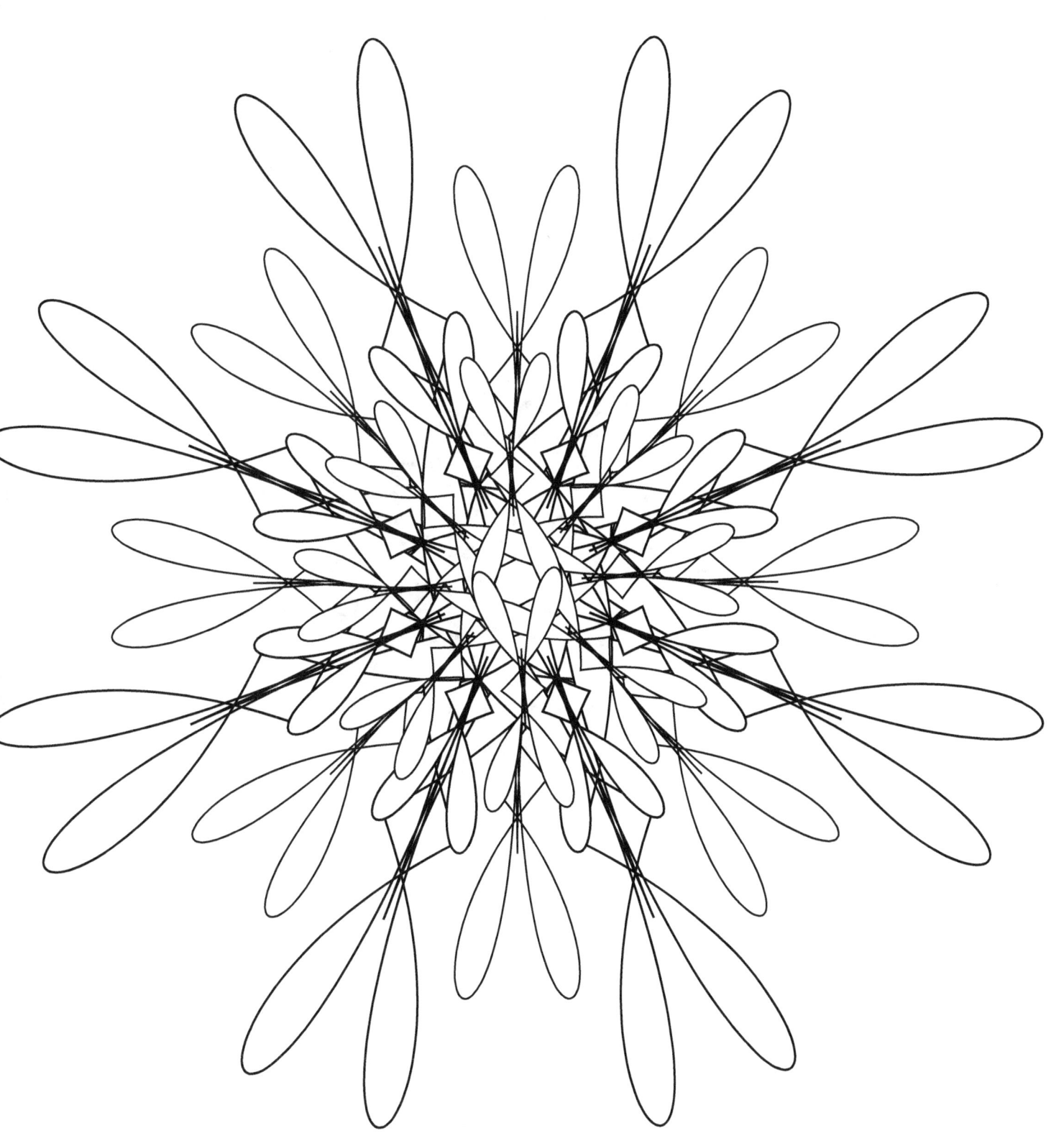

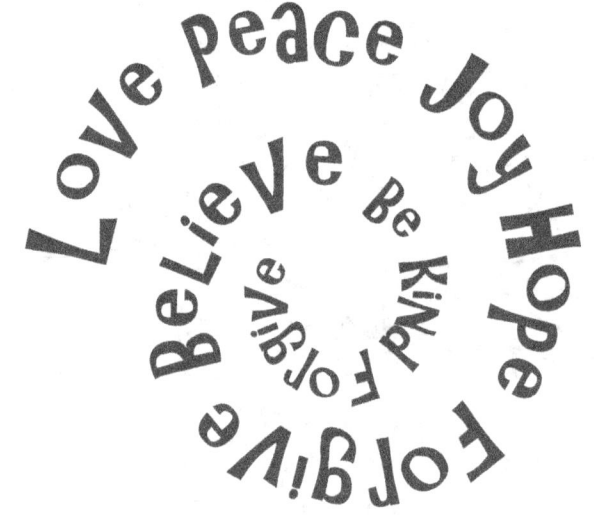

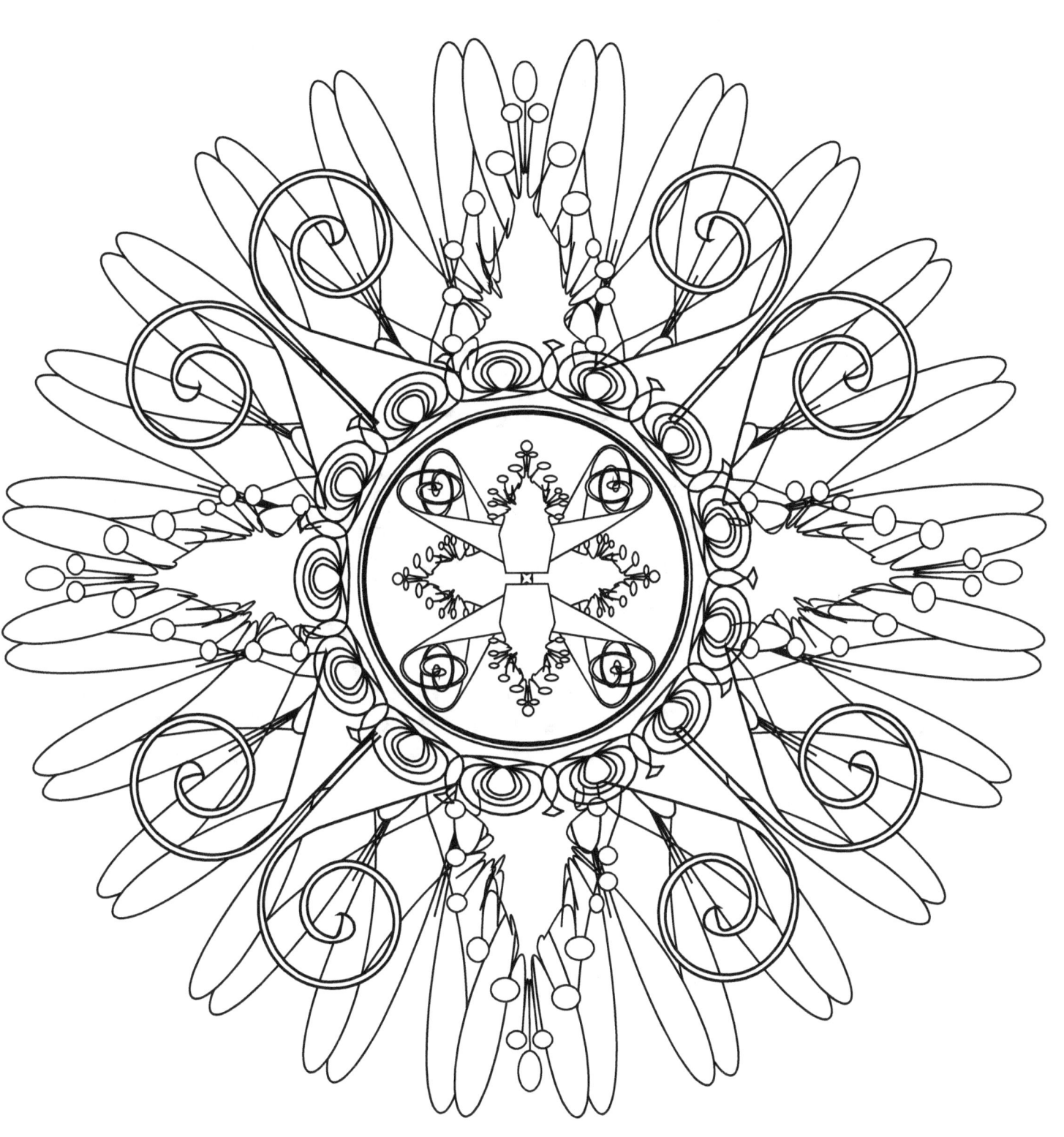

Shine Bright Shine Bright Shine Bright Shine Bright Shine Bright Shine Bright Shine Bright

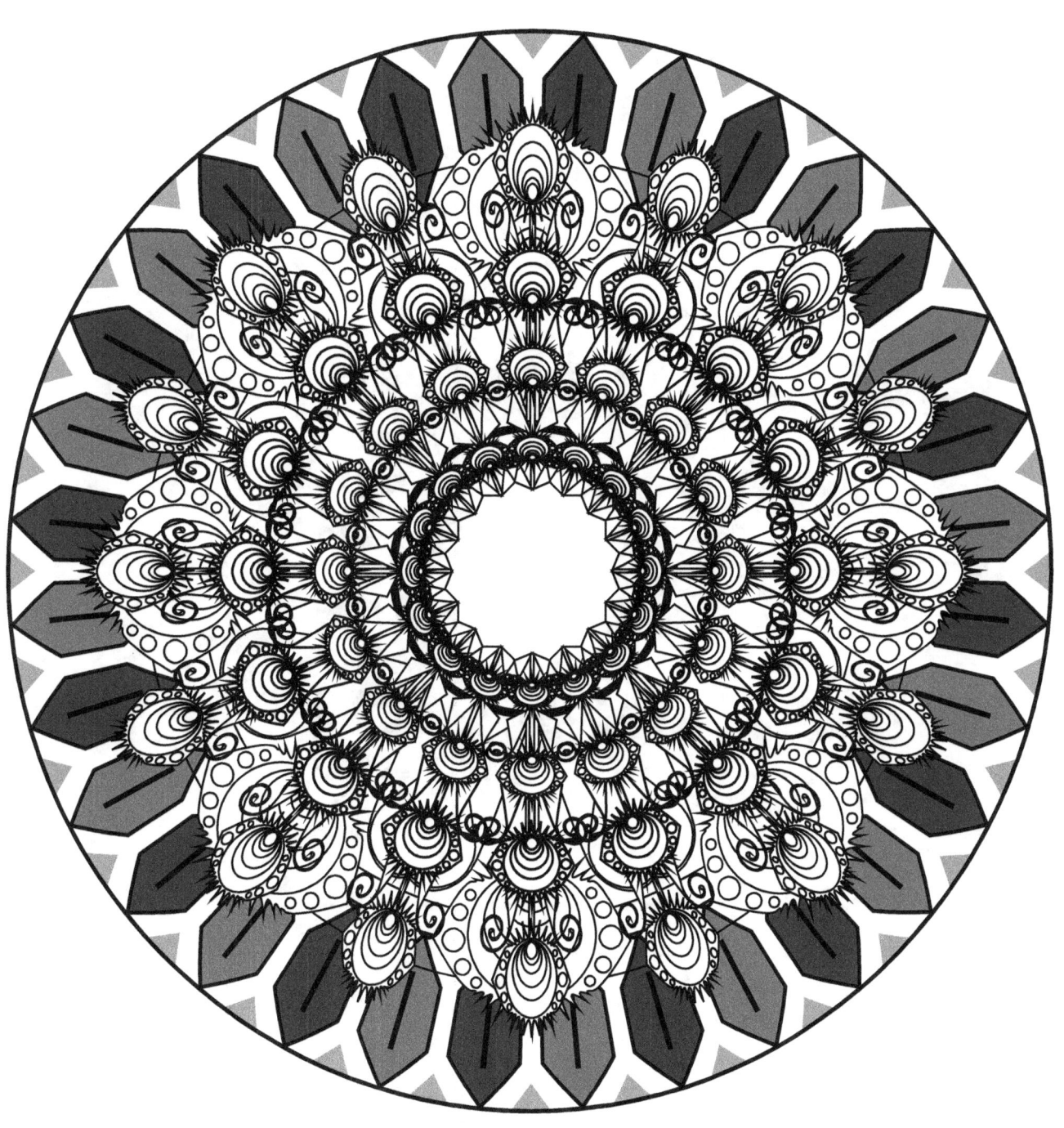

PRAY PRAY PRAY PRAY PRAY PRAY PRAY PRAY PRAY PRAY

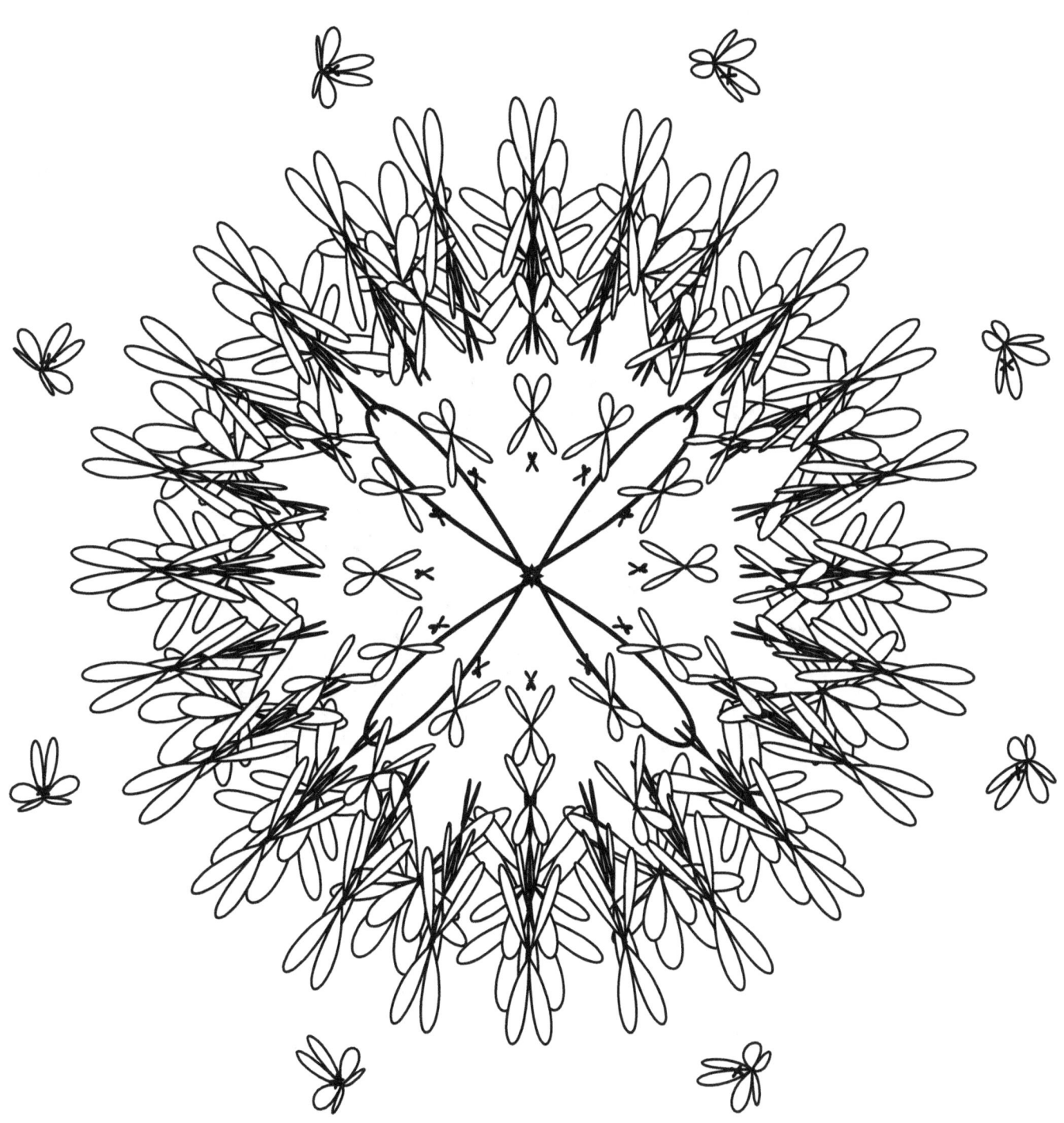

Art Heals the Soul Art Heals the Soul the Soul the Art Heals Art Heals the Heals the

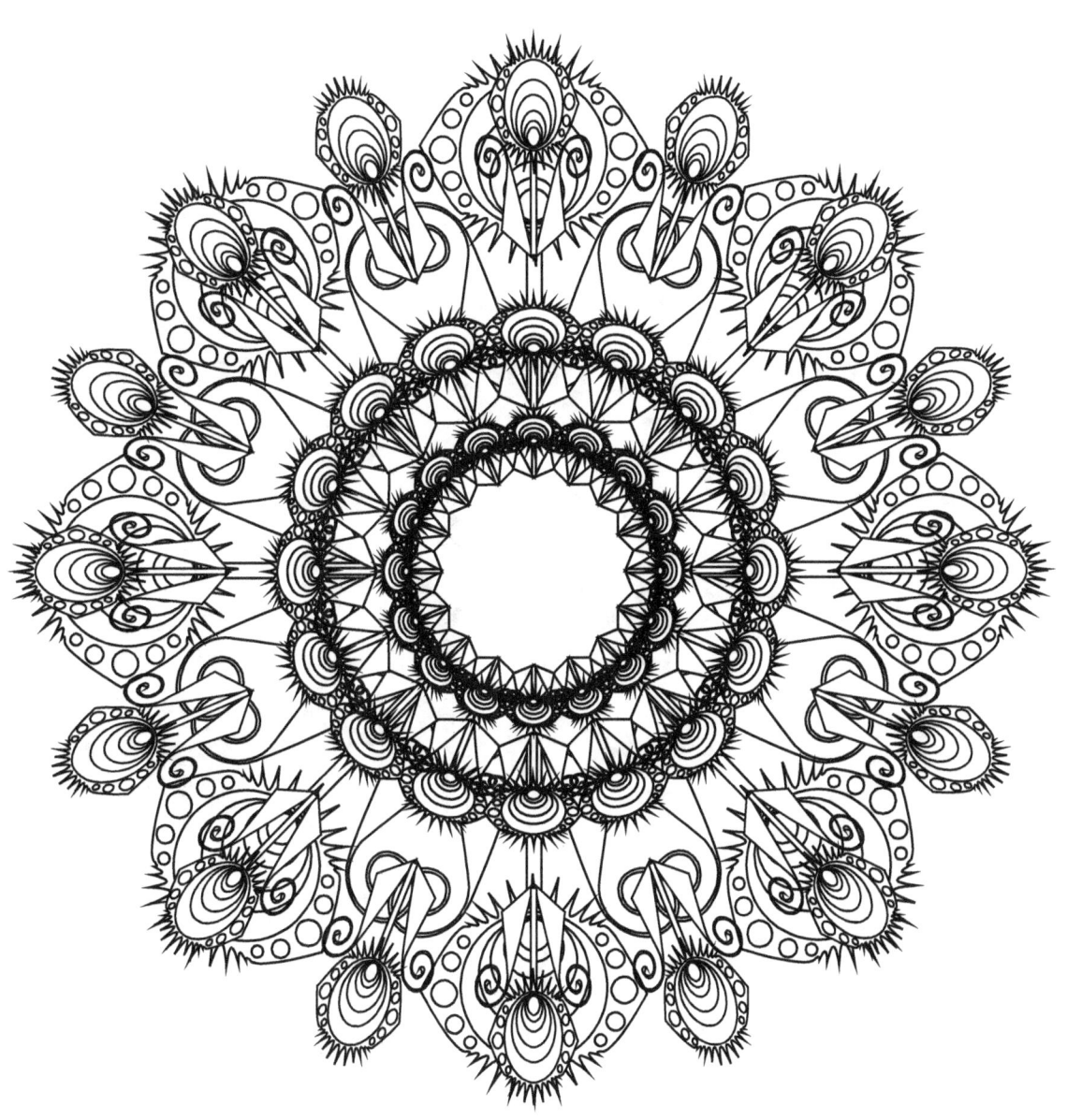

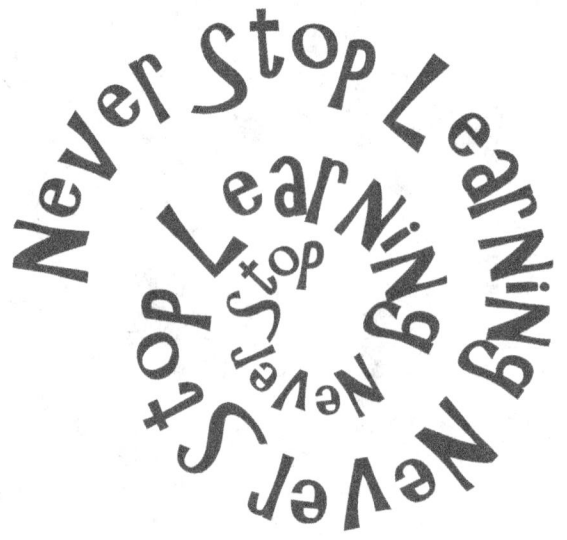

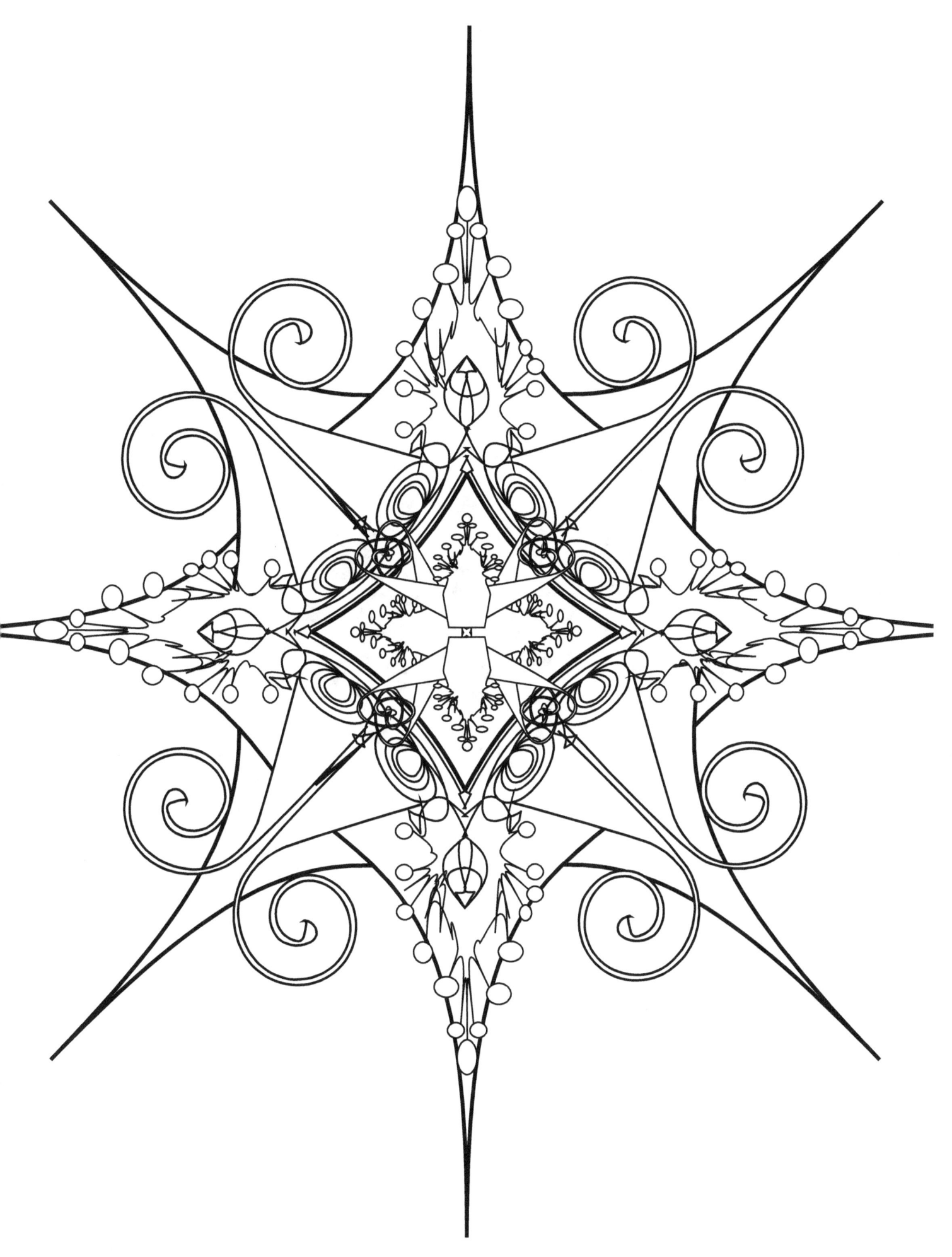

Be Still and Know Be Still and Know Be Still and Know Be Still and Know Be Still and Know

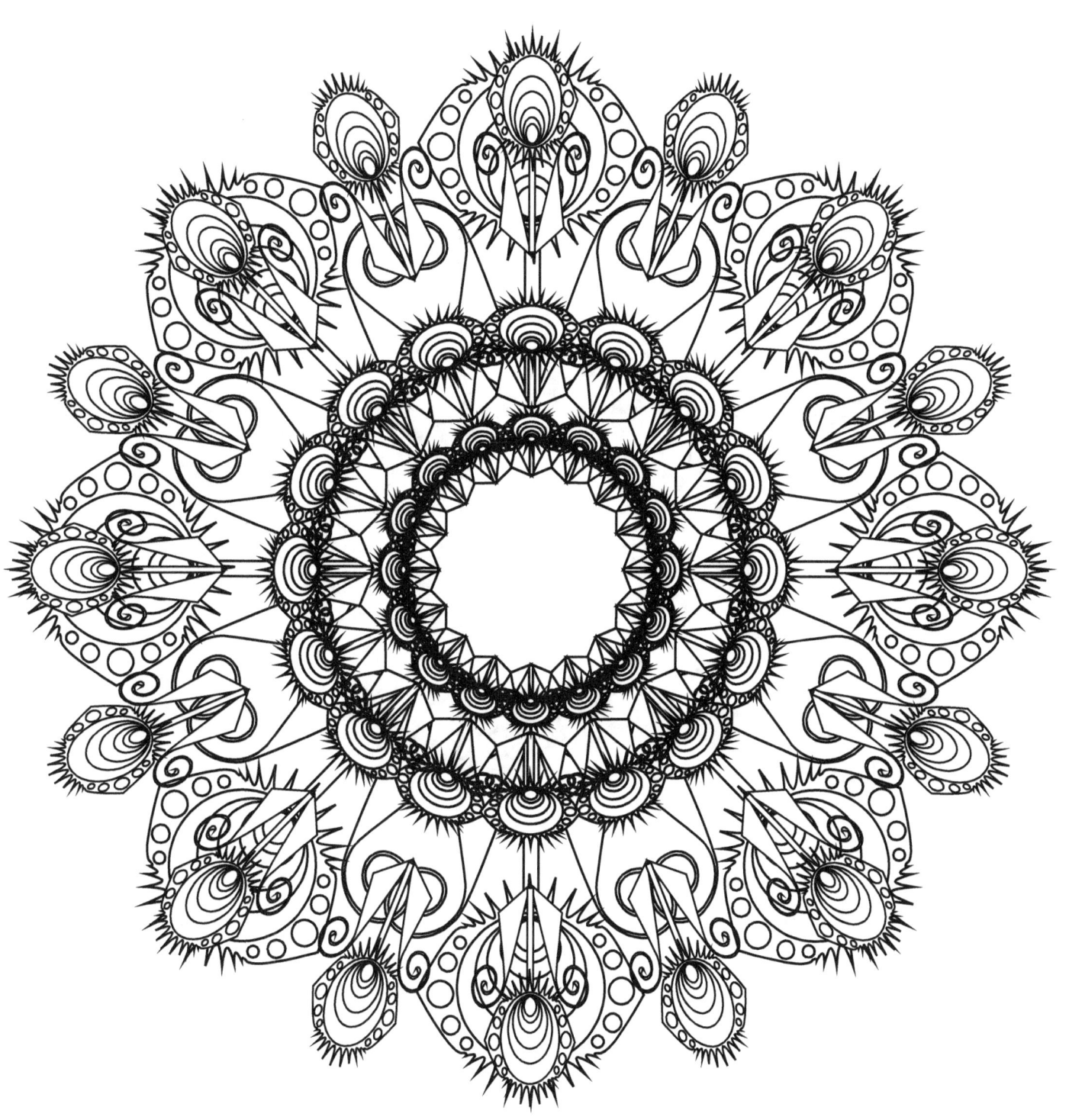

Create Create Create

Create Create

Create

Create

Create

Create

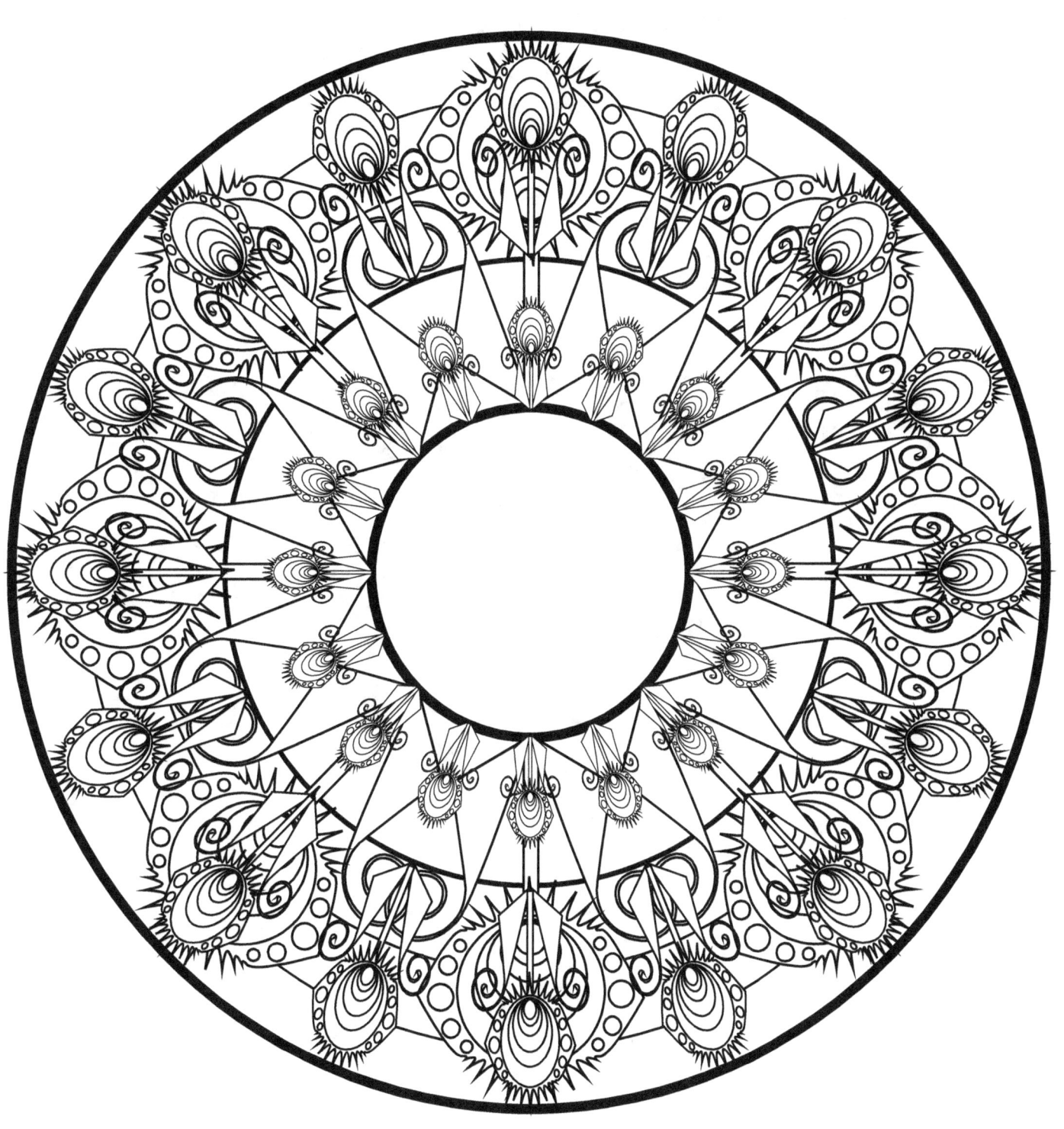

Let your Light SHiNe Let your Light SHiNe Let your Light

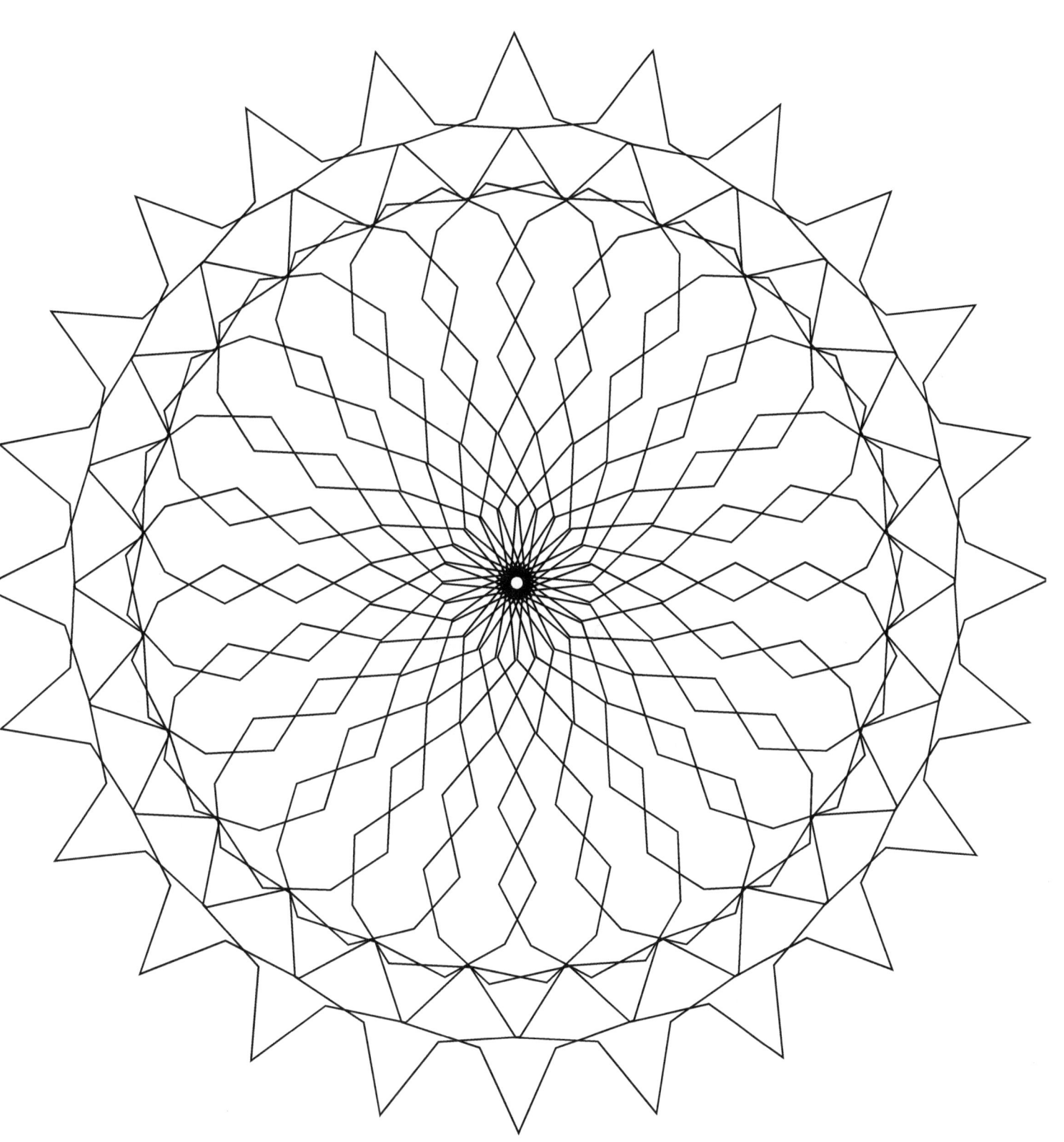

BeLieVe BeLieVe BeLieVe BeLieVe BeLieVe BeLieVe BeLieVe BeLieVe

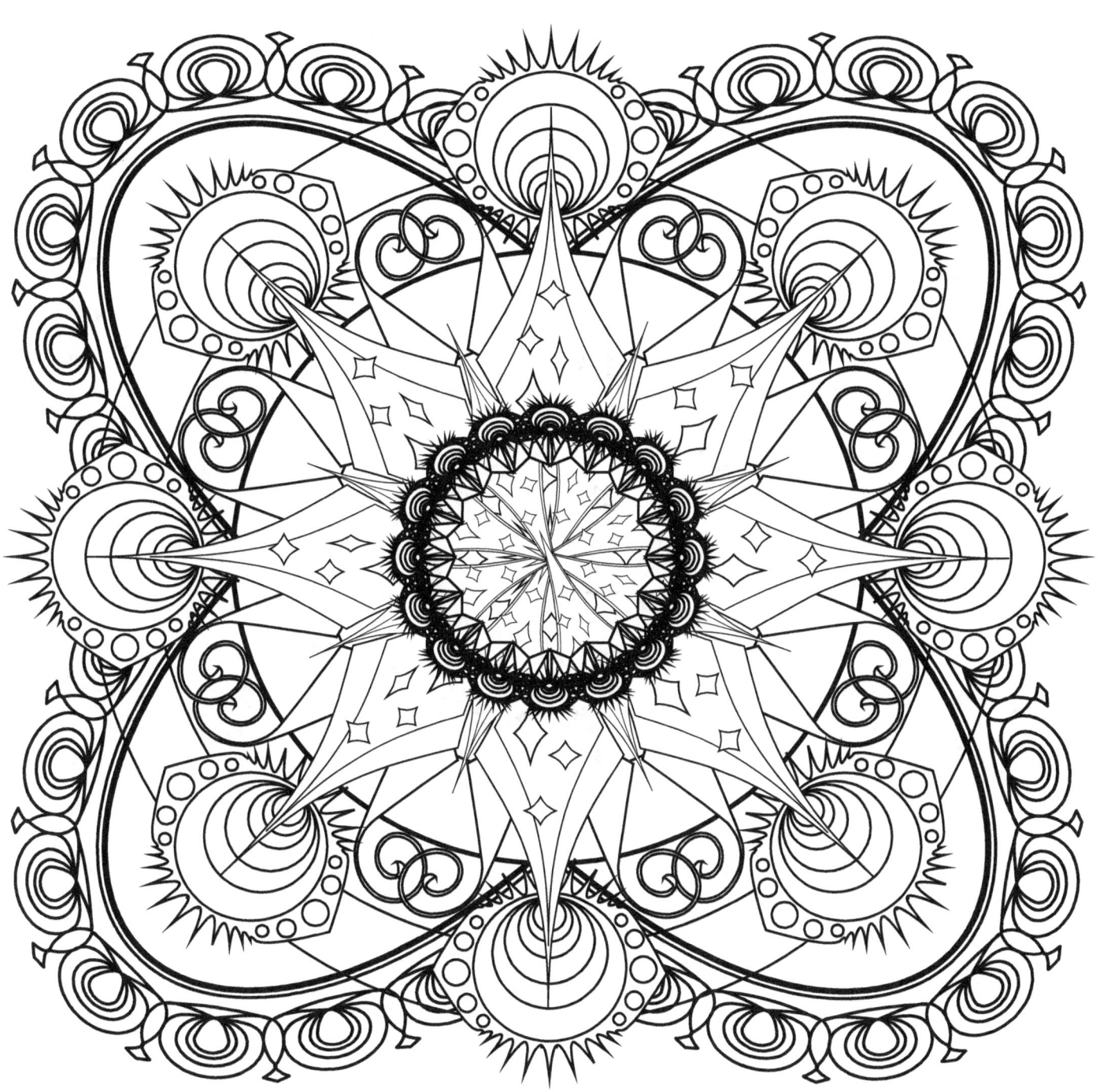

Laugh often Laugh often Laugh often Laugh often Laugh often Laugh often

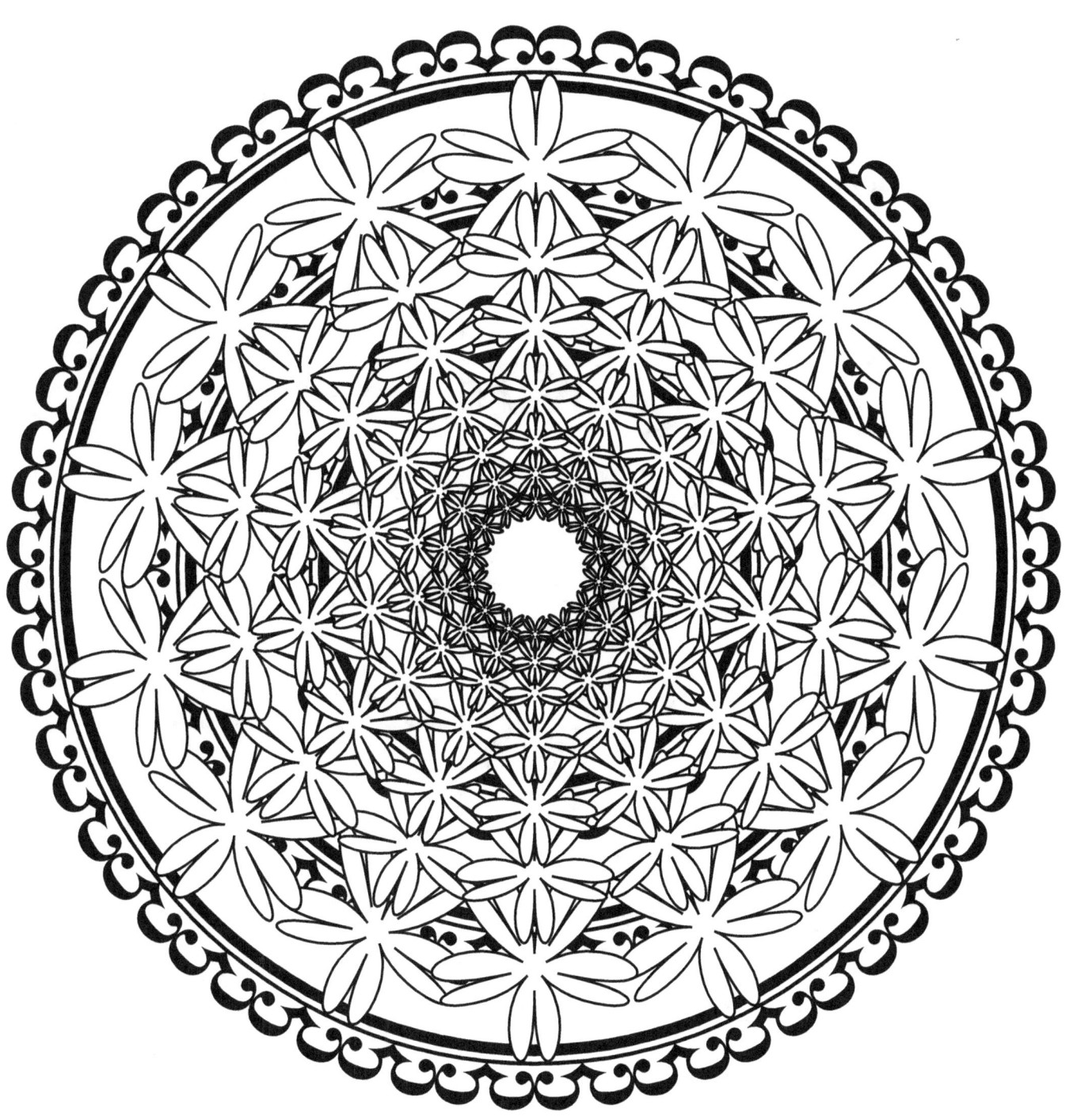

SHe BeLieVed SHe CouLd So SHe did

SHe BeLieVed SHe CouLd So SHe did

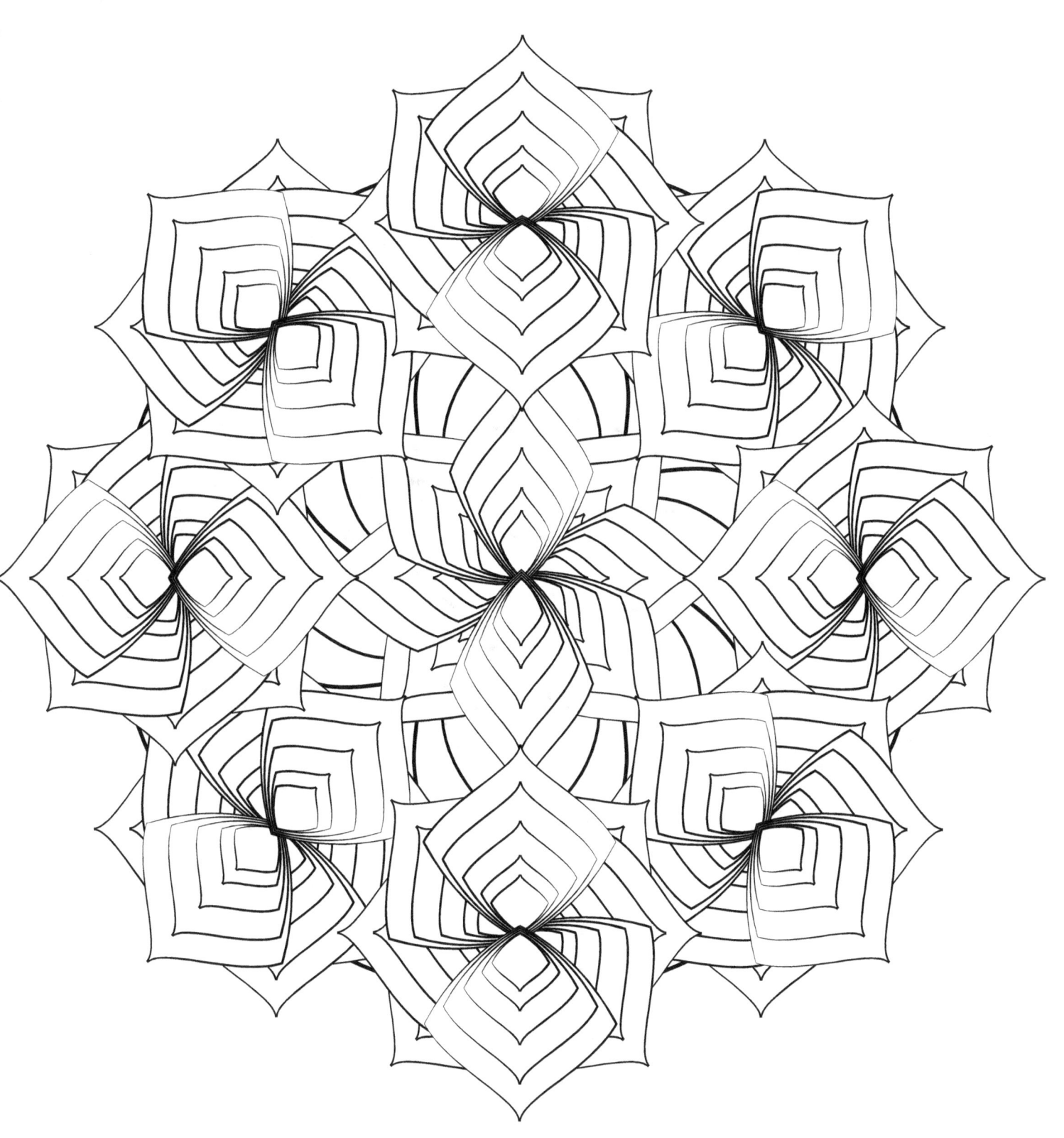

Dreams Do Come True Dreams Do Come True Dreams Dreams Do Come True Dreams Do

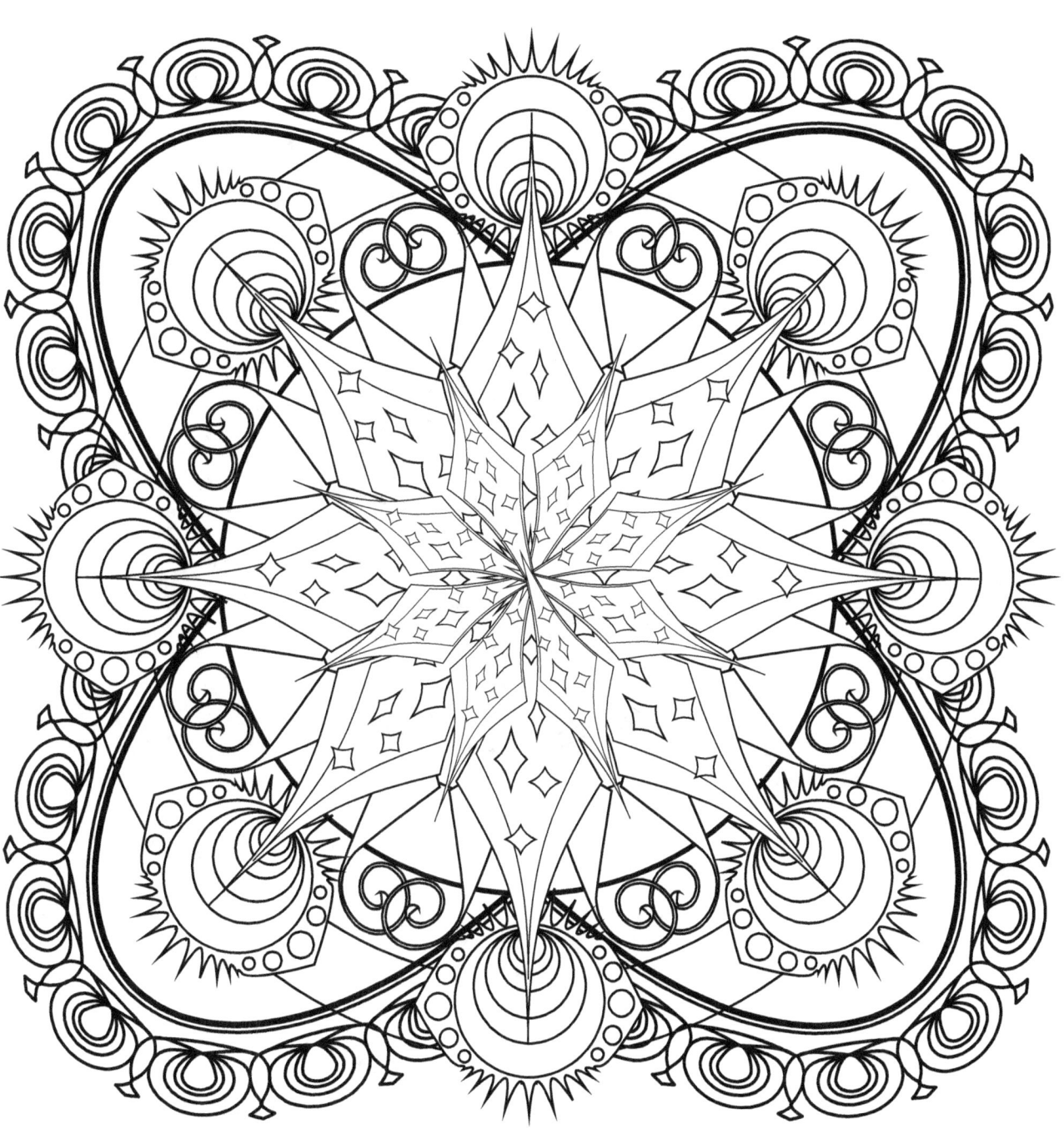

Believe iN YourSeLF Believe iN YourSeLF Believe iN YourSeLF Believe iN YourSeLF

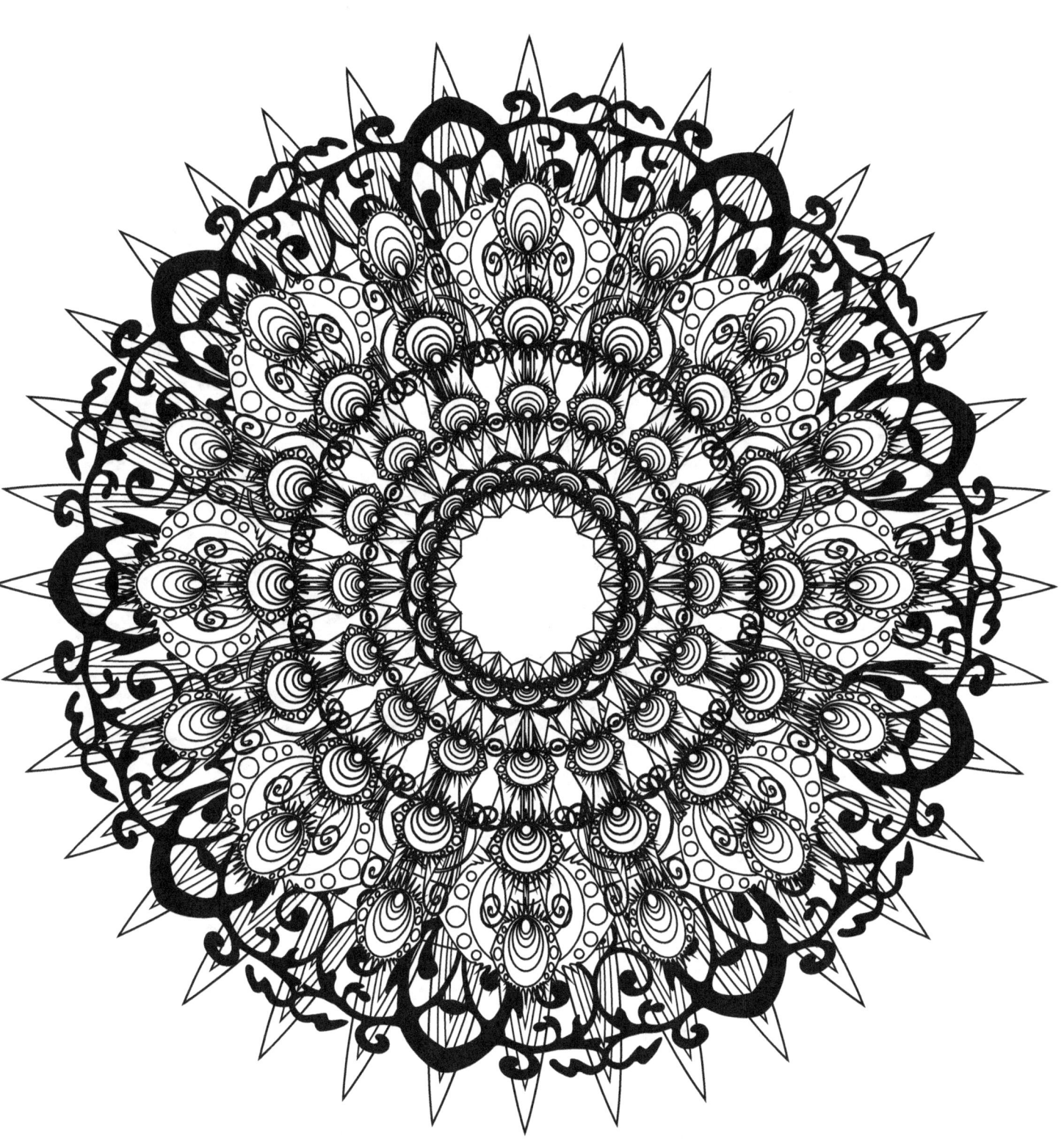

Live your passion Live your passion Live your passion Live your passion Live your passion

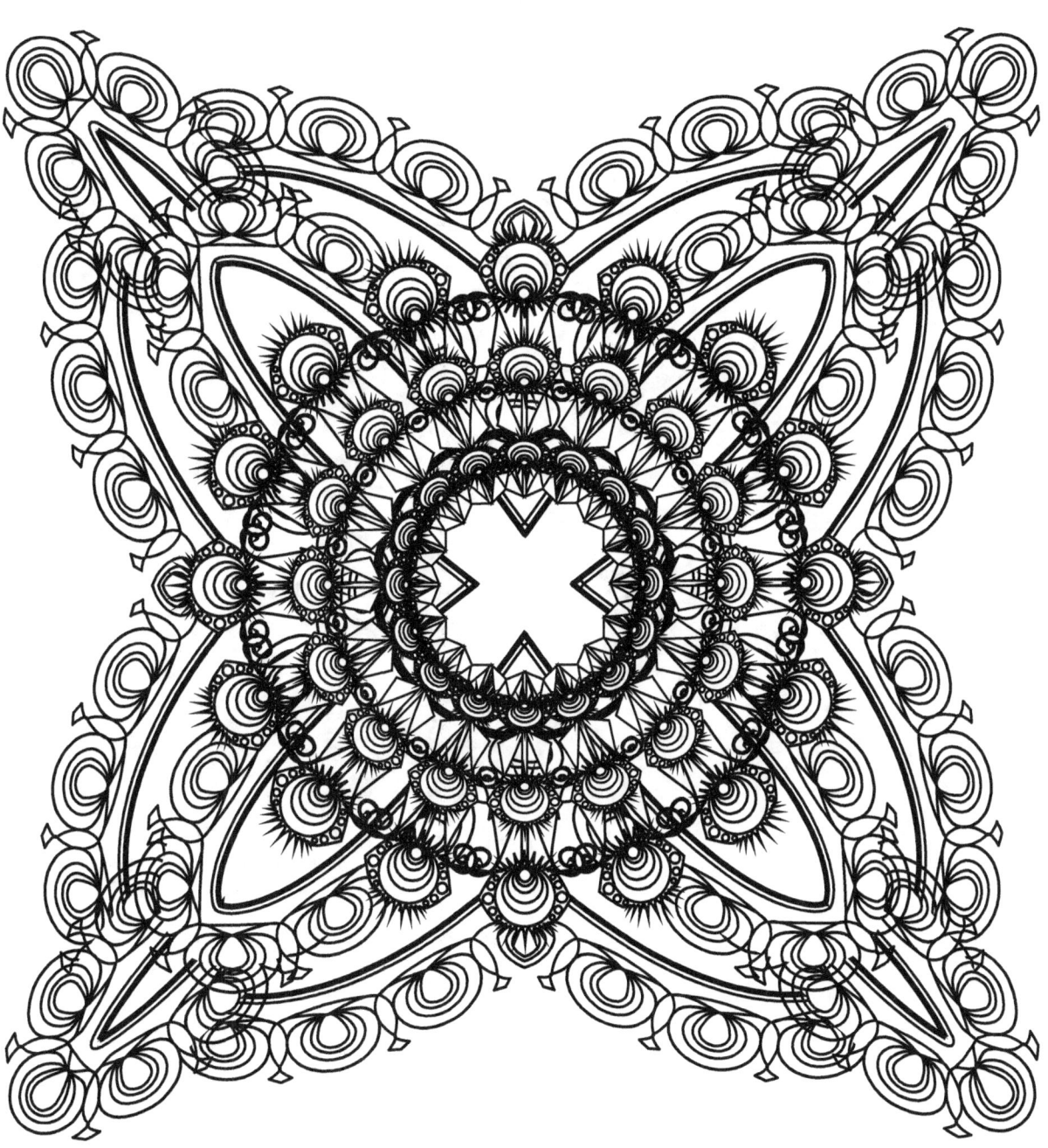

Celebrate everyday Beauty Celebrate everyday Beauty Celebrate everyday Beauty

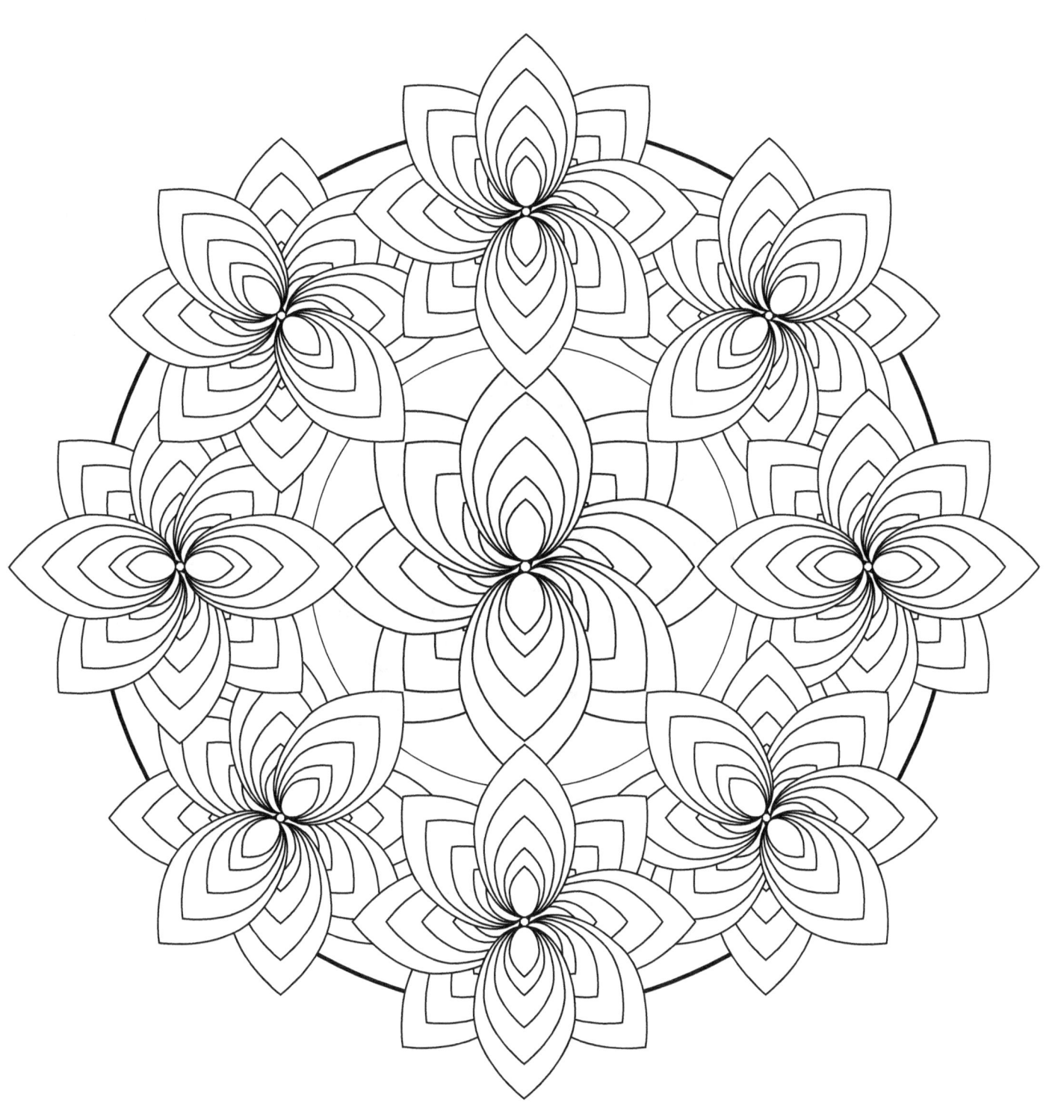

Be Bold! Be Bold! Be Bold! Be Bold! Be Bold! Be Bold! Be Bold!

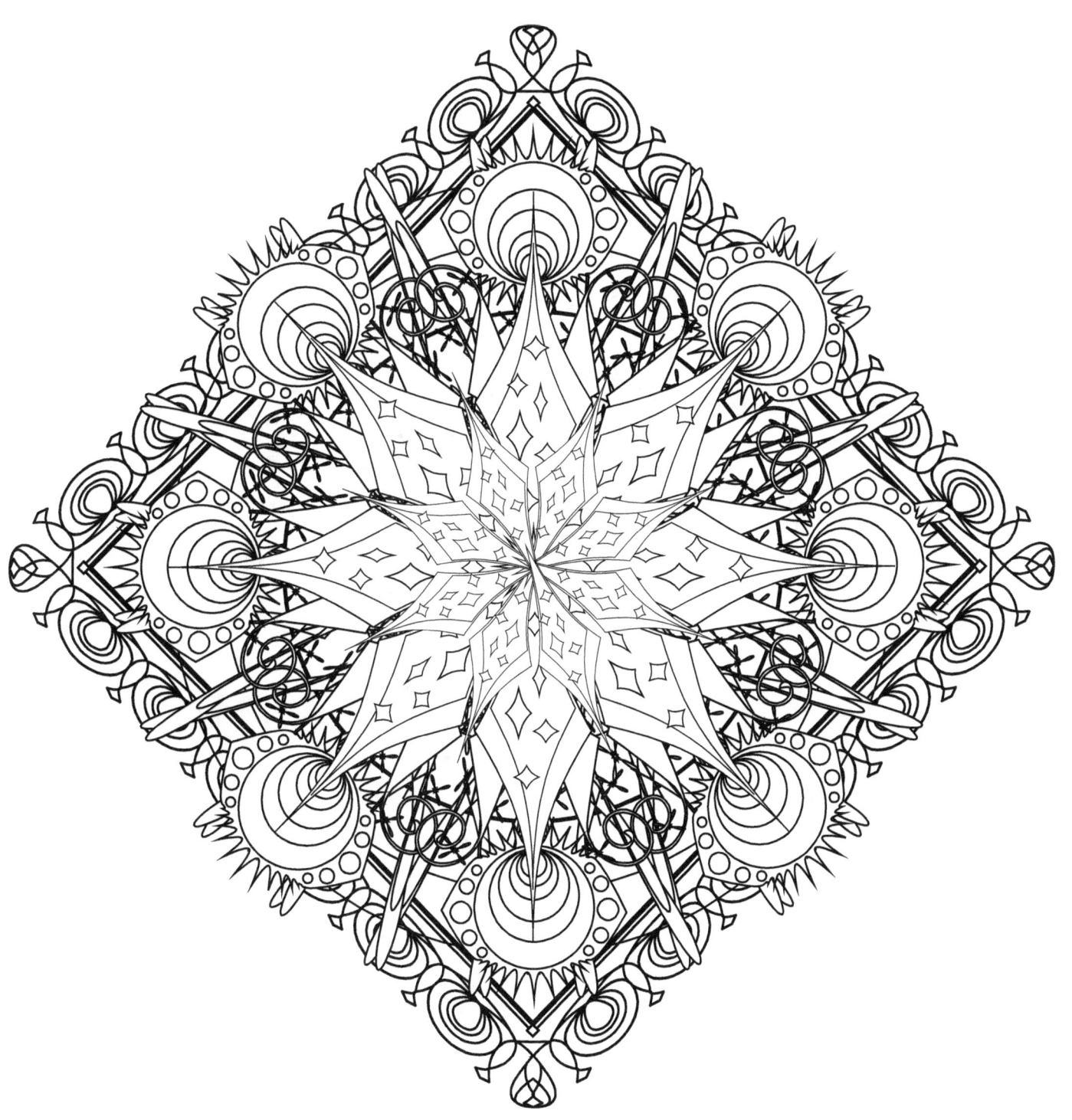

Live Fully Live Fully Live Fully Live Fully Live Fully Live Fully

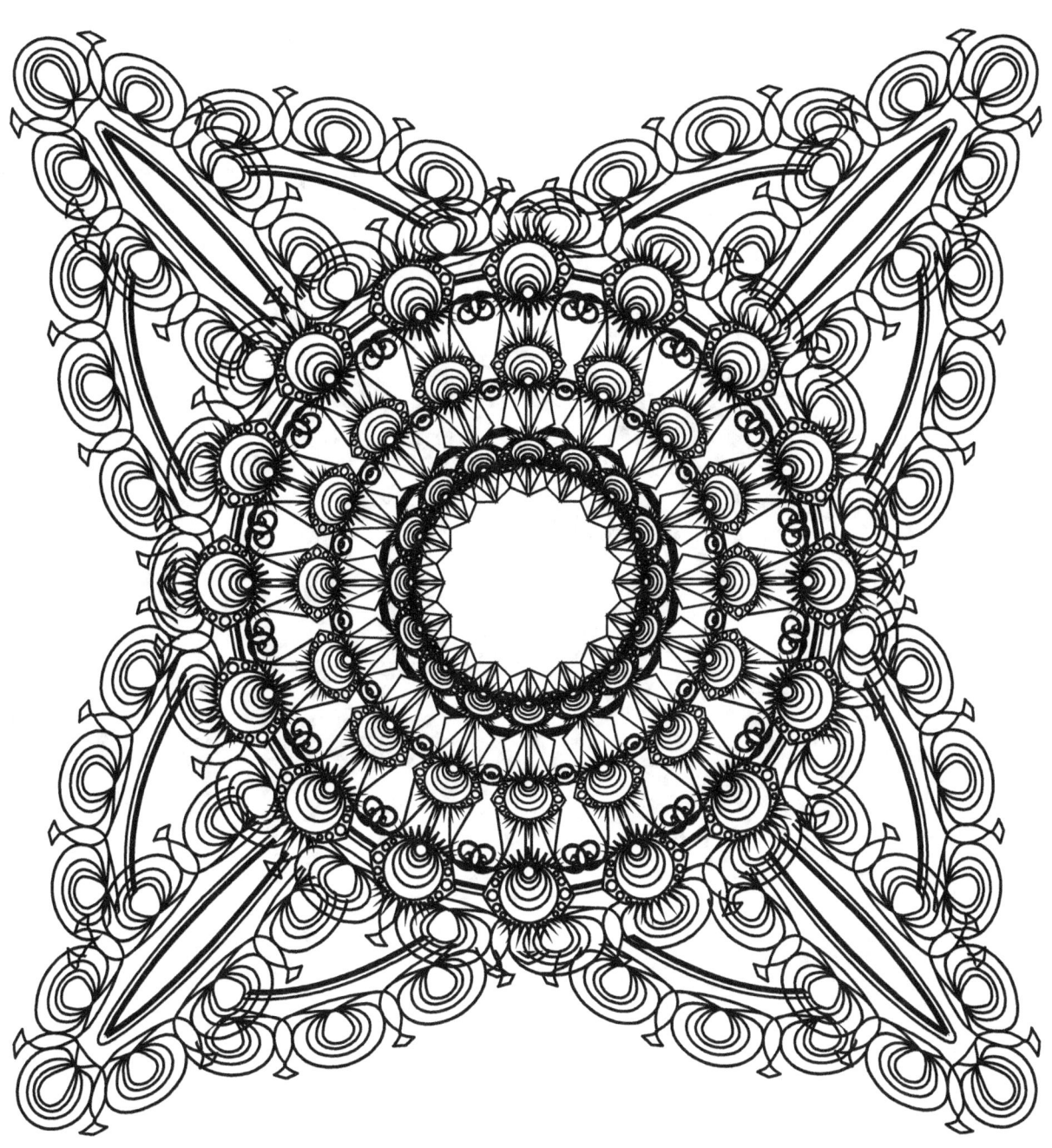

Laugh often Laugh often Laugh often Laugh often Laugh often

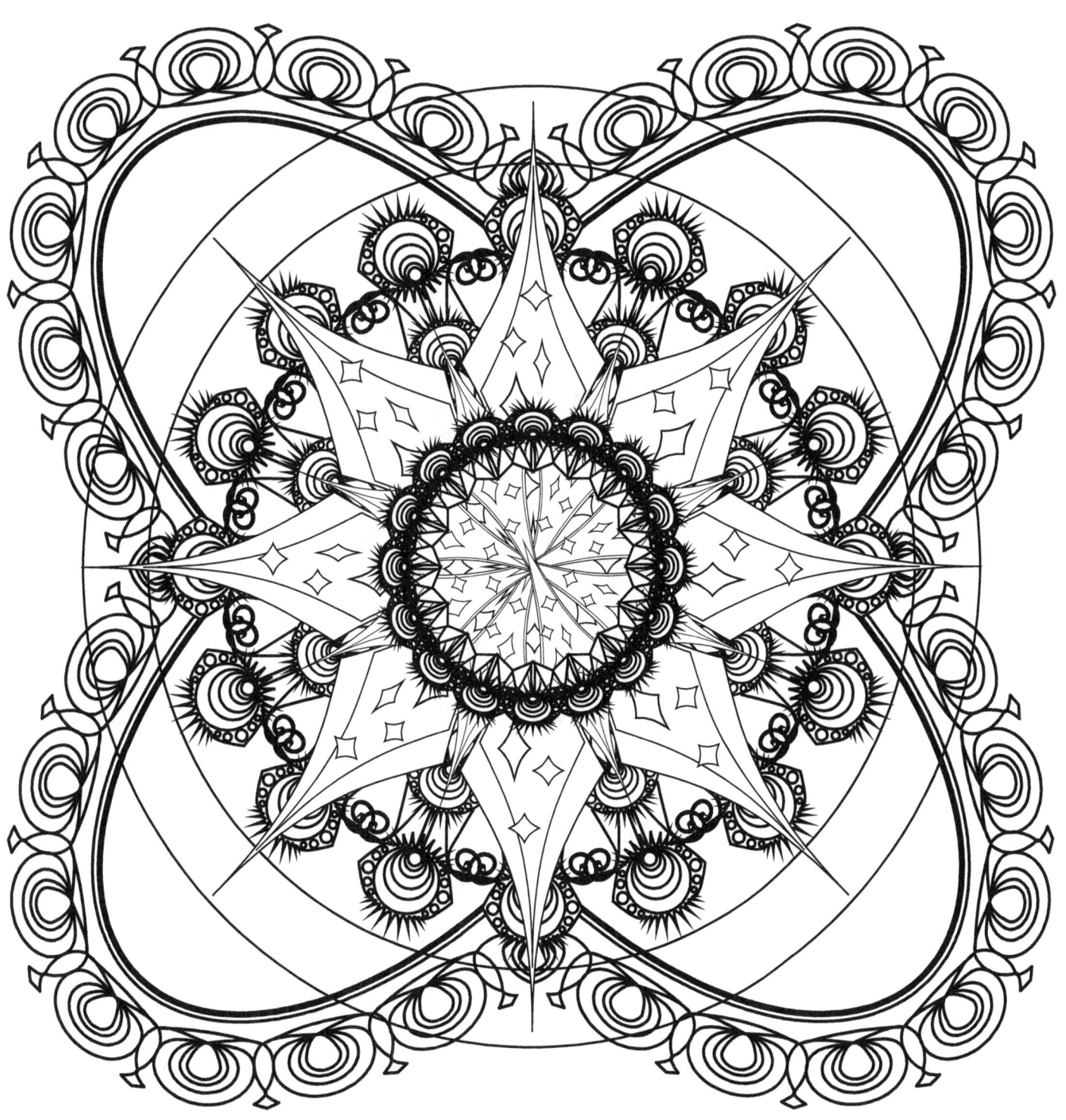

JOY JOY JOY JOY
JOY JOY JOY
JOY JOY
JOY
JOY
JOY JOY
JOY JOY JOY

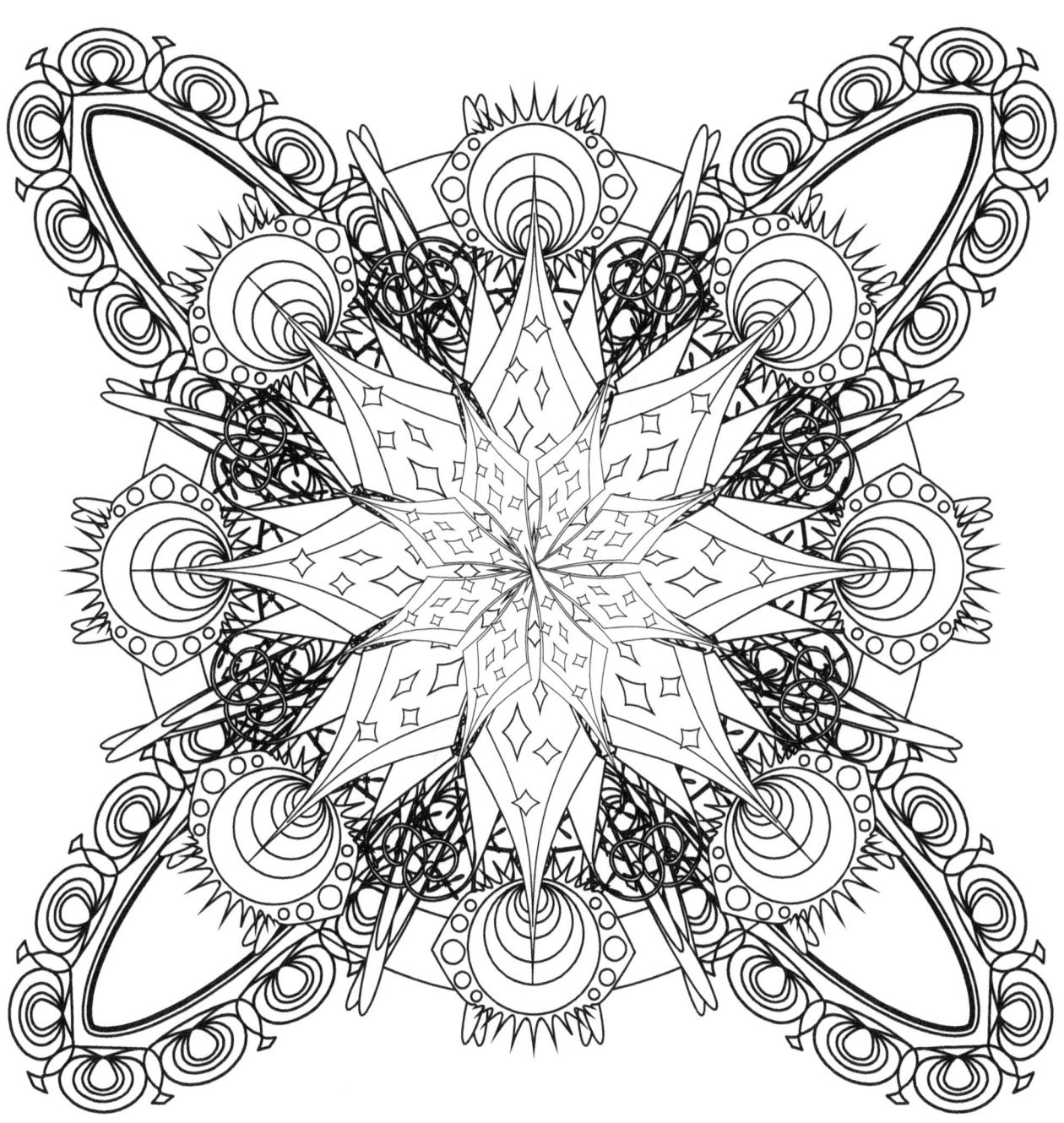

Forgive Forgive Forgive Forgive Forgive Forgive Forgive Forgive

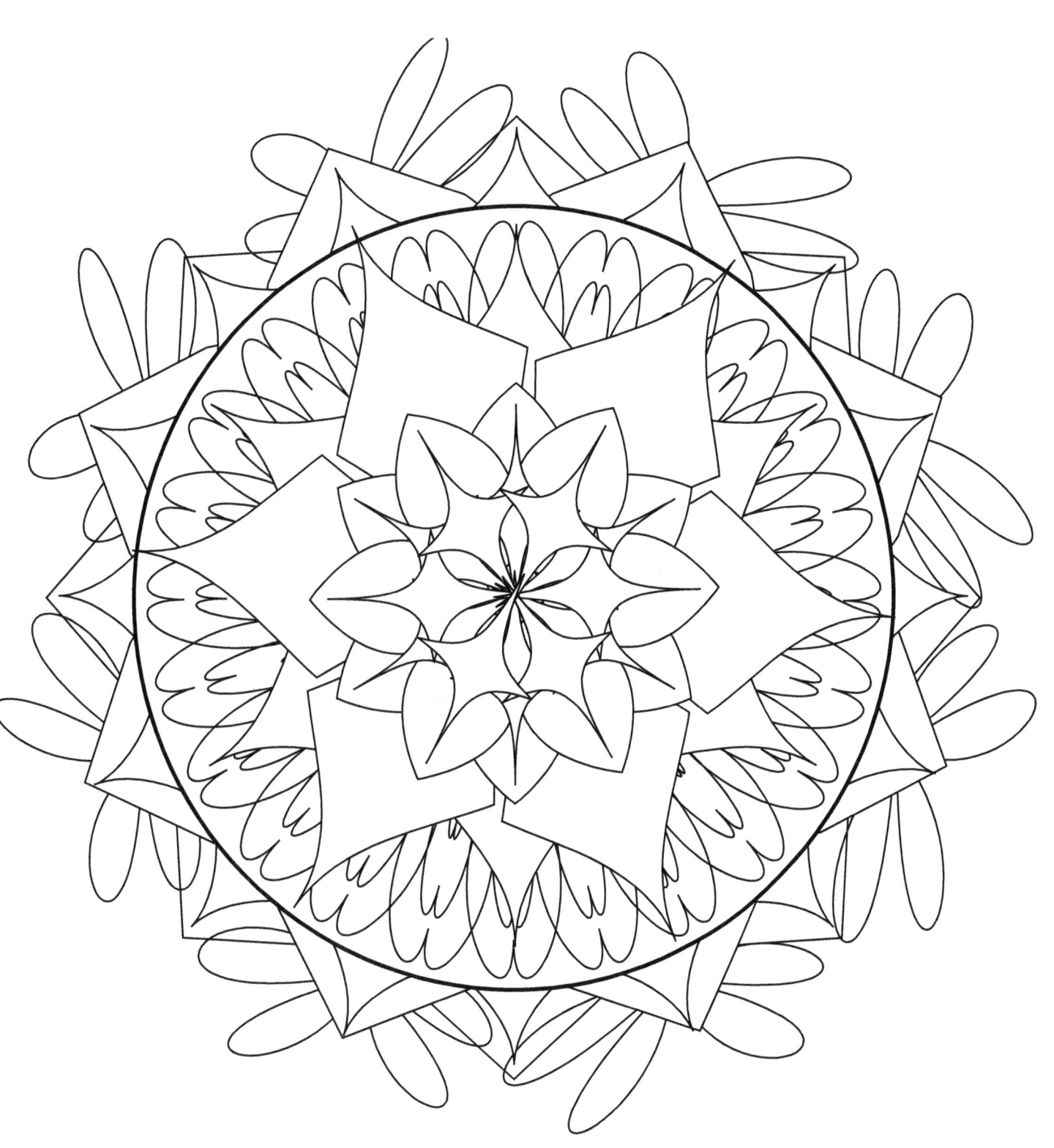

Help Others Help Others Help Others Help Others Help Others

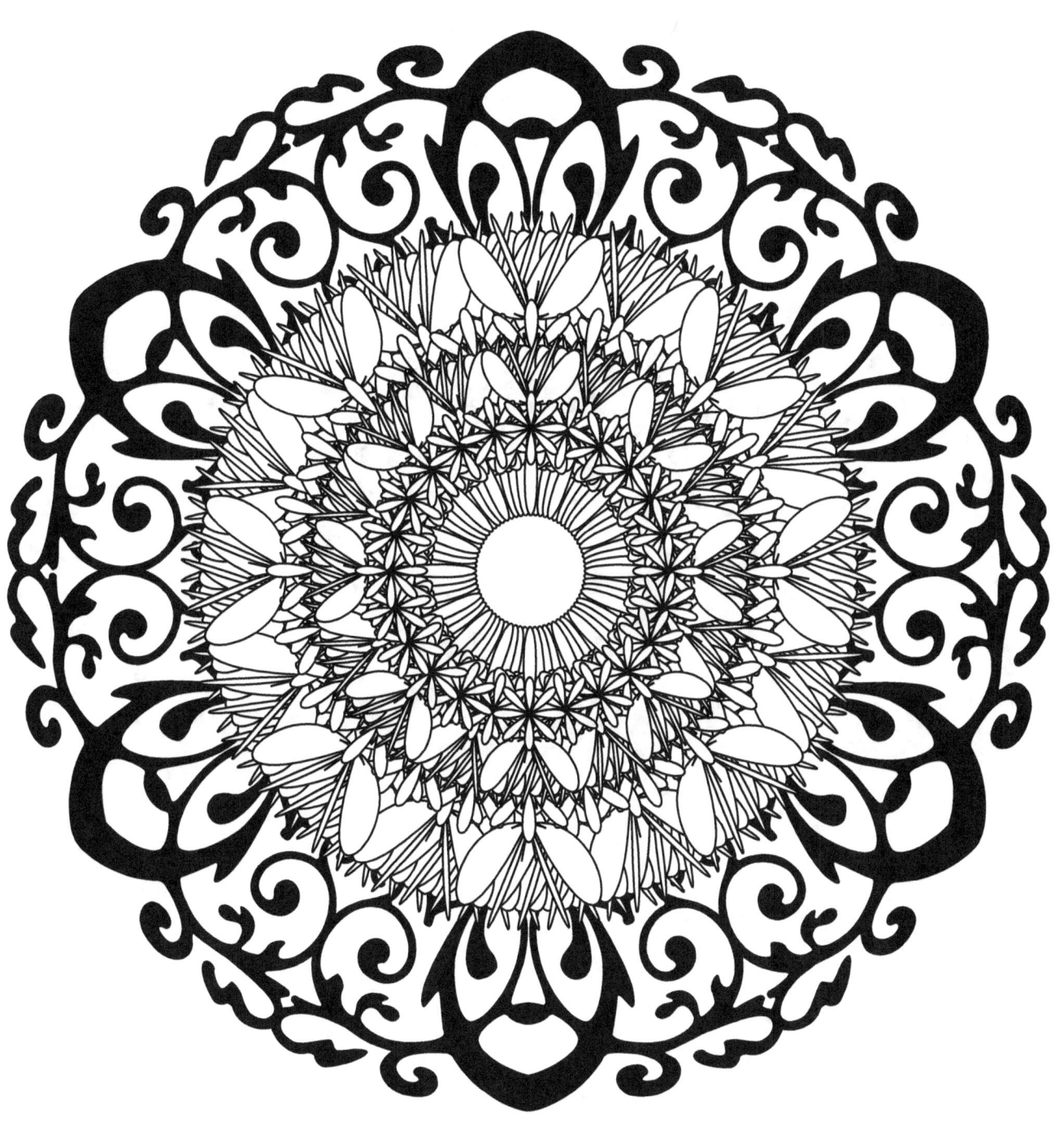

Live Laugh Love Live
Laugh Love Live
Love Live
Love Laugh
Laugh Love

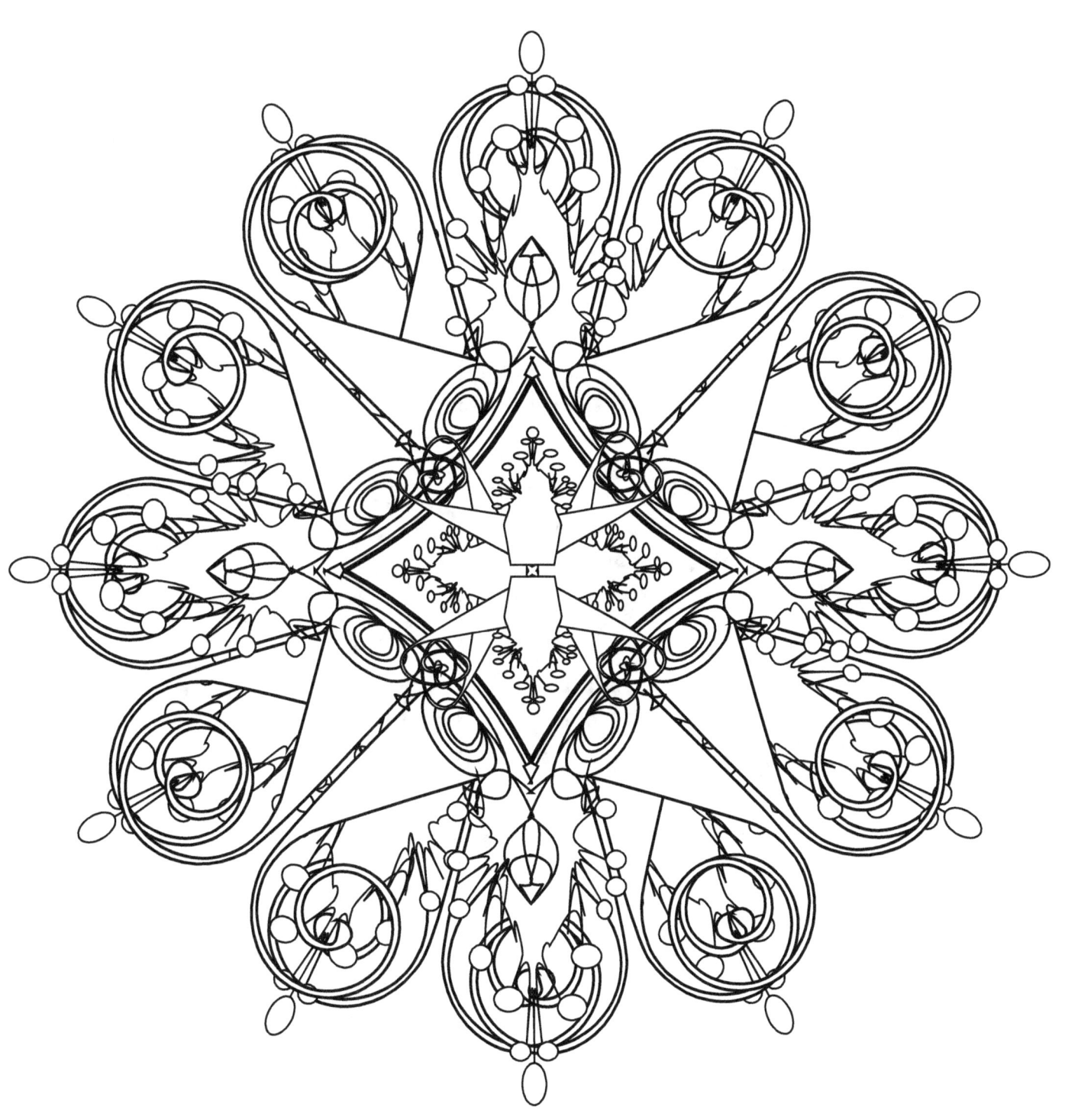

Forgive Others Forgive Others Forgive Others Forgive Others Forgive

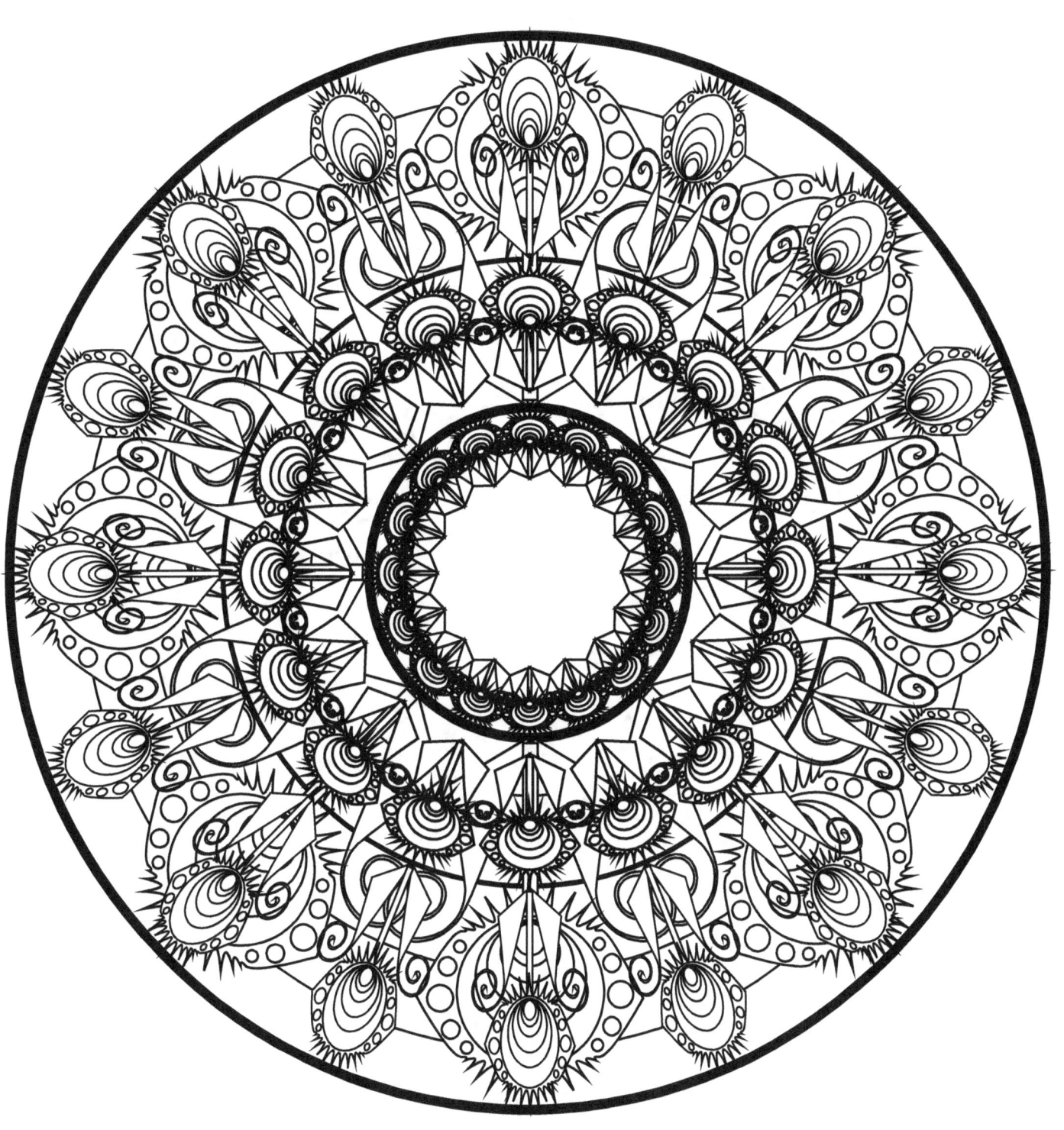

Live FULLy LiVe FuLLy LiVe FULLy LiVe FuLLy LiVe FuLLy

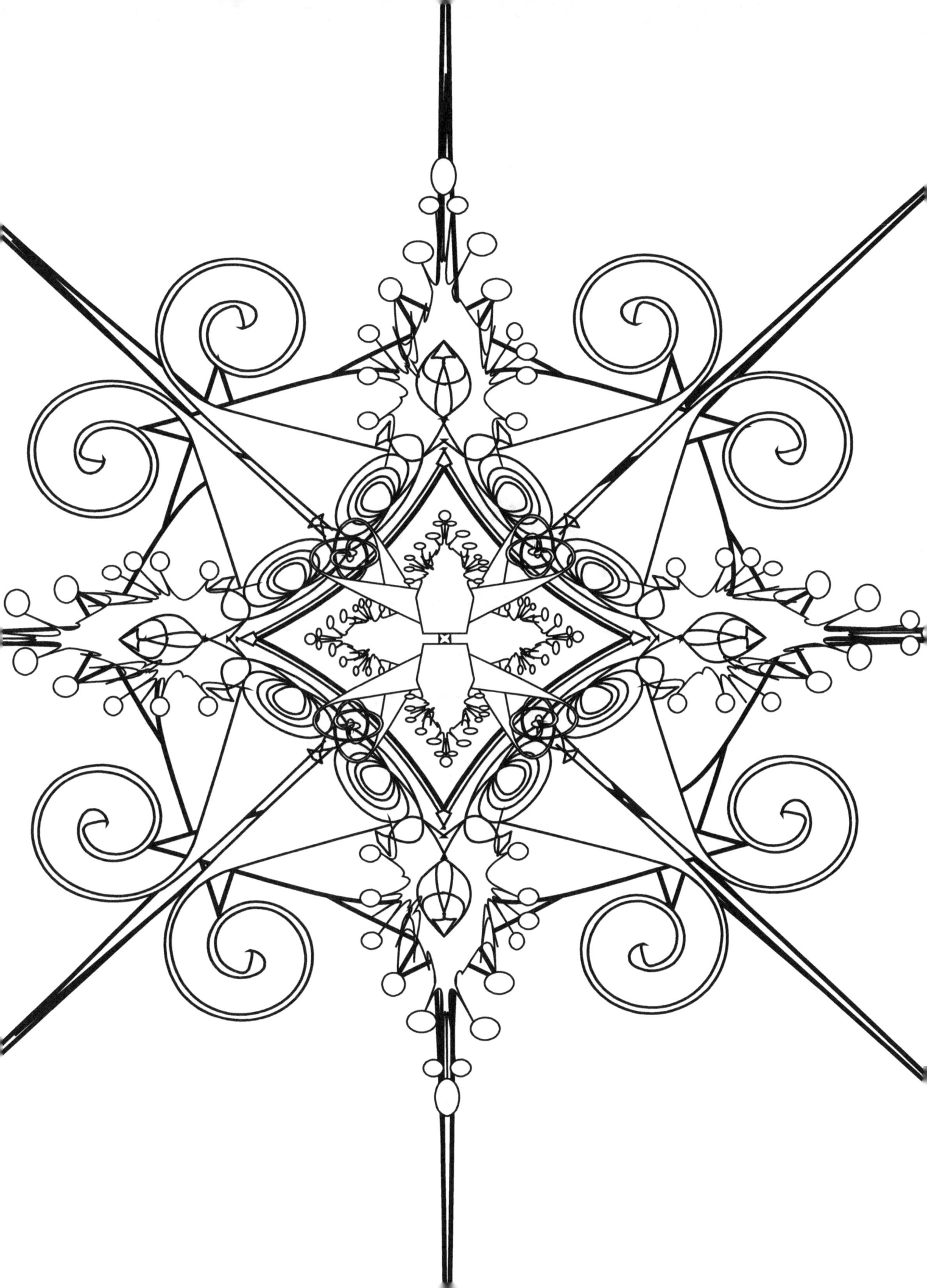

Let your Light SHiNe
Let your Light
Light SHiNe
Light
Let your

www.ingramcontent.com/pod-product-compliance
Lightning Source LLC
Chambersburg PA
CBHW081200180526
45170CB00006B/2160